# Girl in Blue

# Anne Ramsay

with Diane Taylor

# Girl in Blue

How One Woman Survived
Fourteen Years in the Police Force

MACMILLAN

First published 2008 by Macmillan
an imprint of Pan Macmillan Ltd
Pan Macmillan, 20 New Wharf Road, London N1 9RR
Basingstoke and Oxford
Associated companies throughout the world
www.panmacmillan.com

ISBN 978-0-230-70902-7

1 3 5 7 9 8 6 4 2

A CIP catalogue record for this book is available from
the British Library.

Typeset by Intype London Ltd
Printed and bound in the UK by
CPI Mackays, Chatham ME5 8TD

Visit www.panmacmillan.com to read more about all our books
and to buy them. You will also find features, author interviews and
news of any author events, and you can sign up for e-newsletters
so that you're always first to hear about our new releases.

*For my dad*

# *Acknowledgements*

I'd like to thank the following people. My mum, who is my rock, for the love and encouragement she has always given me. Lesley Gordon and Graeme Hind for their humour and for helping me to believe in myself. Edel Godwin and Mariette Hardman for always being there. Tom Paterson for his help and advice. Jim Wilson who started the ball rolling. Elizabeth Sheinkman, my agent, who had faith in the story and made it possible. Richard Milner, Stephanie Sweeney, Lorraine Baxter and especially Ingrid Connell, my editor at Macmillan, for all their guidance and support. And finally Diane Taylor for all her hard work and dedication. What started off as a working relationship turned into a true friendship.

## Author's Note

This is a true story and the events I'm describing all took place. However, with the exception of my family, many of the names and the characterizations have been changed to protect the innocent.

# Girl in Blue

# Prologue

'You'll get a lot of business tonight.' He eyed me up with a mixture of disdain and lust.

I glanced down at my luminous turquoise trousers, so tight that they clung to my thighs, and pressed my head against the dirty window pane. It was cold. The door closed behind me and I was alone.

I stared down at the traffic below, mesmerized by the bright lights bouncing off the grubby pane of glass, then took a step back and felt the cold air on my skin as it forced its way through the badly fitted window frame. The wind was so powerful that I could see the flakes of paint dance off the walls of the dingy room.

I tried to pull the matching crop top down towards my trousers, but the skimpy material wouldn't stretch far enough. I reached for the black leather jacket that was hanging on the old armchair. It was borrowed from a friend and I'd been warned I'd better not lose it. Then I locked the door and headed out.

The biting wind lashed at my face as I made my way towards the drag and I was glad I'd managed to put a pair of tights on underneath my trousers. Some of the girls were standing in little huddles and a few were by themselves. I felt anxious because of the recent murder. I could see my breath in front of me, steam that turned to ice when it hit the air. As I approached my patch at the clock tower a few of the girls slipped into punters' cars. They had struck lucky.

I leaned back against the cold brick wall underneath the huge clock. A girl standing close to me was giving me dirty looks. She was shivering with cold and her painfully thin legs dangled from her miniskirt.

I smiled at her but she glared back.

'This is ma bit,' she shouted across to me. Her two front teeth were missing. Rather than get into a fight I moved away. There was room enough for everybody.

I watched as the same cars drove slowly past me then around the block and back again, looking for girls. A black hatchback was heading in my direction and slowed down. The insistent, heavy baseline of rave music blared out. There were two men inside. Most girls wouldn't go with two men because it was too risky. I moved quickly away from the pavement – I'd heard of girls being snatched – then made my way towards the safety of the wall under the clock tower and the car sped off.

# One

An image of Margaret Thatcher flashed up on the TV, talking about the merits of privatization. I was sitting at home watching the news with my mum and dad. My dad, a man with a passionate sense of fairness, began shouting at the TV. 'Privatization my arse!' he growled. 'She's just a money-grabbing cow making the rich richer and the poor poorer.'

He was cut off mid-rant by the sound of the phone ringing. The three of us glanced at each other. We were all looking forward to watching our favourite soap after the news and nobody wanted to get involved in a long phone conversation.

'You're nearest, you get it,' my dad said to me.

'I'm not getting it, I don't want to miss *Crossroads*. You get it and if it's for me say I'm out.'

'You get it, Anne,' my mum said. 'If it's your aunty Roseanne tell her I'll phone her back after *Crossroads*.'

I jumped up and answered the phone irritably.

'Hello.'

'Oh hello. Is that Bernadette Ramsay?' said a clipped voice.

'Well, I'm known as Anne,' I said. 'Nobody ever calls me

Bernadette, at least nobody since the school nurse when I was five.'

'Right. It's Inspector Robertson here from Deanspark police station. I'm calling about your home visit. I'm on my way up to you now.'

'OK, that's fine, no problem,' I said in a much more enthusiastic tone of voice than the one I'd answered the phone in.

'Oh shit,' I said to myself.

I'd recently returned from three years working in Germany, first in the hotel and catering industry then in the airline business, and had applied to join the police. The process took six months and involved a medical, an exam and a home visit announced at short notice, if any, so that applicants could be seen as they really were without having time to put on a show.

I rushed into the living room. *Crossroads* had just started and my mum and dad were sitting on the settee with their eyes glued to the screen.

'Quick,' I shouted urgently. 'That was the police on the phone; the inspector's on his way up here now for the home visit.'

My mum looked panic-stricken, all thoughts of watching the telly vanished.

'I don't know if I've got anything in to give him with a cup of tea. And look at the state of this house. George, help me clear these plates away. I'll get the Hoover out.' She sprang into action at the speed of a Tasmanian Devil.

My dad was much less anxious about making a good impression and was annoyed at having his viewing interrupted. He didn't move.

'For God's sake I'm watching this. They pick their times. Can't they come another day?' he said.

'Yeah, right, Dad, I'll just call them back and see if they'll do that. Are you daft? We're lucky to get a phone call. Sometimes they just turn up.'

'I don't know what you want to do that job for anyway. That's no job for a woman, it's far too dangerous,' he sighed. When he realized that there was going to be no chance of watching *Crossroads* he got up off the settee.

'Stuff that, I'm off to the pub,' he said, brightening at the prospect. I was relieved that he'd decided to go out. My dad was a straightforward working-class man who always called a spade a spade. If he'd stayed to see Inspector Robertson he would probably have said to him exactly what he'd just said to me. Dad reached for his jacket. Even though he was only going down to the local pub he liked to look smart and took pride in his appearance. He was a trim five foot nine, and kept fit by walking everywhere. He'd never lost the good physique he'd built up in the army more than thirty years ago. His blond hair was thinning but his twinkling blue eyes and cheeky grin were as lively as they'd always been.

My dad was a real people's person and had the gift of the gab. He was very sociable and always full of fun. Well respected by his friends and neighbours, he had become a local hero when he rescued a neighbour's three-year-old son from drowning, receiving a medal from the Lord Provost. He did his apprenticeship as a shipwright for Stevens of Linthouse, a big Glasgow shipbuilding company, after he left school. At the age of twenty-one he carried out his national service and joined the Royal Electrical and Mechanical Engineers, where he worked as a mechanic. Most of his time in the army was spent abroad in places like Tripoli. At the end of his national service he received a glowing report. The colonel who wrote it called him 'a bit of a character'.

He returned to his trade when he left the army and got a job at the shipyard, where for a while he was working alongside Billy Connolly. But he was made redundant so he started working with my uncle running outdoor markets up and down the country.

As a little girl I was a real tomboy, always clambering up trees in my old jeans, and unlike most girls of my age I had friends who were boys as well as girls. We used to race each other and play football and I made sure that the boys never beat me.

From the age of eight my dad took me with him to Yoker Market at weekends, which wasn't too far from where we lived. My dad's job was to collect the rental money from the stallholders and to make sure that the market ran safely. This was a perfect job for him, because he was very sociable and was on first-name terms with all the stallholders. He had a reputation for treating everyone fairly and was renowned for having a laugh. Going to the market with my dad was always a thrill for me: because everyone loved and respected him I was treated like a little princess. If I went to the fruit stall I was given a bag of fruit, if I went to the sweets stall I came away with a handful of my favourite black jacks or fruit salads. My dad let me count out the money he'd collected, which made me feel very grown up and responsible, and was always delighted when I did the sums correctly. Christmas was a particularly magical time. Dad bought lots of presents cheaply from his stallholder pals and I was in heaven as I sat absorbed in the riches he showered on me – colouring books, felt-tipped pens and cuddly toys.

My mum was much quieter than my dad and held everything together at home. She really lived for her children and worked wonders to make sure my older brother, my two older sisters and I had everything we wanted. Although we weren't well off I never felt poor and we were always nicely turned out. As well as being practical Mum could be very creative, and quite often we had things that were a bit different from other kids. She found me a blue silk tie to wear as part of my school uniform instead of the nylon bobbly one that everybody else was wearing.

She was small and slim, with lovely glowing skin and dark eyes. She had a heart of gold and would give up her last penny for someone else. As a young woman she'd worked for Singers, the sewing machine factory in Clydebank. She left work to marry my dad and became a housewife. Kim was born first, four years later James came along, Lynne arrived two years later, and a year and a half after that I was born.

As I rushed to get ready I suddenly remembered something my mum had told me when she'd worked as a part-time cleaner at the Strathclyde Police headquarters. She started work early in the morning and often found empty whisky and vodka bottles in the bins, something that shocked her. When she worked nights she sometimes witnessed the parties held in the police station on Friday evenings. She told me that some of the bosses got very drunk, tried to chat up young female office staff, then rolled off to drive themselves home. I was shocked by this but assumed that the drunken parties at police headquarters were a thing of the past.

One of the least favourite parts of my mum's job at police headquarters was cleaning the basement. There was an old museum there with wooden stocks, a heavy moleskin suit which had been worn as a punishment, opium pipes in glass cases, and old-fashioned weapons. Mum would have to dust around the waxwork dummy of Madeleine Smith, posed in a black high-necked dress, a bonnet on her head. Madeleine poisoned her lover when she was only twenty-two but escaped hanging when the jury gave her a not proven verdict. Much worse was the dummy of Peter Thomas Anthony Manuel, a notorious serial killer who was hanged in 1958. A shiver ran down my spine whenever Mum referred to him.

As my mum raced around tidying up the living room and stowing dirty plates and cups out of sight in the kitchen I looked down at the jogging pants I was wearing and thought, 'There's no way I can meet him like this . . .' So I rushed upstairs to get changed, flung various items out of my wardrobe, and eventually settled on a white shirt and black jeans.

'It's vaguely like a police uniform,' I said to myself. 'So at least he'll be able to get an idea of what I'll look like in the job.'

All sorts of thoughts were running through my head as I pulled my clothes on. I was feeling apprehensive and wondered if the interview would be like the police interrogations I'd seen on TV. Would Inspector Robertson be coming by himself, or would there be a row of officers lining up on my mum's sofa to grill me?

I wondered too what the inspector would make of our house. It was a modern, end-of-terrace, three-bedroomed council house on the Summerston Estate and we'd lived there since I was three. It was brand-new when we moved into it, built on what used to be open fields before the council decided to put houses there. To me it felt enormous because it had a front and back garden. The flat we'd moved from had an outside toilet, while this house had a bathroom and toilet upstairs and another toilet downstairs. It seemed like a palace. We lived in the northwest of Glasgow, a middling kind of area which was neither good nor bad. There was some crime but there were plenty of worse places to live. Everybody knew everybody else on Summerston and there was an open, friendly atmosphere. We steered clear of the few rough families and saw very little trouble. All the children on the estate grew up together and went to the same school. Kim, Lynne and I slept in the same room, while James had a room of his own. Lynne and I shared a double bed and there were plenty of fights at bedtime over territory. We drew an imaginary line down the middle of the bed and we'd squash right up against each other, bum against bum, to make sure that the other one didn't stray into 'enemy territory'. We must have looked ridiculous, because most of the bed was left completely empty.

I took my hair out of its ponytail and brushed it well. I decided against putting make-up on. I wanted to look professional but not like a dumb blonde, although I discovered later that the dumb-blonde image might have worked better.

As I checked myself in my bedroom mirror there was a loud, decisive knock on the door. It was a sound that I'd come to recognize as a police knock. In the past my brother, a bit spoilt as the only boy in the family, had fallen in with a bad crowd. He started taking drugs, much to the hurt and dismay of my parents, and because of this he had got on the wrong side of the law. So the police had been at the door quite often when I was growing up. I took a deep breath and ran down-stairs.

Mum had worked wonders and the living room looked perfectly clean and tidy. 'Don't let him come in the kitchen, I've shoved all the rubbish in there,' she whispered.

'Don't worry, I'll keep him in the living room,' I whispered back.

She'd been far too worried about getting the house straight to change her outfit, so now she patted her dark hair, smoothed down her jumper and skirt and hitched up her American tan tights where they'd wrinkled a bit at the ankles.

I opened the door to see a fat balding man standing there. I guessed he was in his mid-forties. His face had that mottled, ruddy look that comes from heavy drinking. The buttons of his police tunic were straining against his paunch. He was wearing his police hat and I decided that he looked like a cross between a walrus and a pitbull. My second thought was that he looked as if he had no sense of humour at all.

I smiled at him but he didn't smile back, instead thrusting his hand out for me to shake. I wasn't used to such formality. 'Come in, come in,' I said, leading him into the living room.

My mum appeared from the kitchen, carefully closing the door behind her. 'Hello, I'm Anne's mum,' she said, smiling broadly. She'd put on her best posh accent and I shot her a bemused look, saying silently, 'Why aren't you talking nor-mally?'

My mum always wanted people's approval, but I was much more like my dad and thought that people should take me as they found me.

Once again he extended his hand without cracking a smile.

'Would you like a wee cup of tea or coffee?' she asked him.

'Ay, I'll have a coffee, thanks. Milk and two sugars.'

'No problem, I'll just leave youz to it,' she said, and disappeared into the kitchen.

'Is it just yourself and your mum that's in?' he asked.

'Yes, my dad's just popped out.' I didn't mention that he'd escaped to the pub. 'Have a seat.'

He sat himself down. 'Is it just yourself and your parents who live here?'

'Yes. My older sister Kim's married, my sister Lynne's away at film school in London and my brother James lives with his partner.'

My mum emerged from the kitchen carrying a tray with two of her best cups and saucers. Miraculously she'd found some cakes and biscuits and had arranged them nicely on a plate. She smiled nervously.

Inspector Robertson explained that the purpose of the home visit was to get to know me better. He would compile a report that he would send to personnel, and on the basis of that report a decision would be made about whether or not to accept me at police training school. All my hopes were pinned on how this man might perceive me.

'Why do you want to become a police officer?' he asked, meeting my eyes intently. A roll of fat from his double chin rested importantly on the collar of his jacket when he looked down at the clipboard he was carrying.

Applying for a job in the police was something I'd thought about a lot. I answered truthfully.

'I think I'd make a good police officer,' I told him. 'I'm good with people. I went to Germany for three years after I left school and worked with lots of different people from different countries there. I'm twenty-one and think I'm quite mature for my age. I feel I've had a bit of life experience. And I'm quite streetwise. Growing up in this area means that I haven't led a sheltered life, although I've never been in any bother myself.'

'How's your general fitness?'

'I go running every morning. I've always been fit. My mum used to say she never saw me because I was playing a different sport after school every day of the week. My PE teacher told me I was talented and a good team player, and I won lots of competitions in hockey and badminton.'

He nodded approvingly. I glanced at his paunch and wondered when he'd last run round a playing field.

'I see here that you didn't stay on to do your highers. What did you do when you left school?'

'When I left school all I was being offered was YTS [Youth Training Scheme] jobs for £24 a week. My dad had always told me those jobs were slave labour set up by Margaret Thatcher to get young people to work for buttons, and I agreed with him. The first job they offered me was in a cheap supermarket. When I turned that down the offers started getting better. Next they offered me one in a bank. I felt I could do better than that and started writing off for jobs off my own bat. Intercontinental were opening a hotel in Glasgow and made me an offer of two different jobs based on my letter. My first job in the restaurant gave me a wage of £120 a week – not bad for someone of my age. I'd always wanted to travel and I managed to get a transfer to one of their hotels in Germany.'

'Tell me more about your work in Germany,' he said.

I explained that I'd been a housekeeping supervisor for an Intercontinental hotel in Frankfurt. It was a huge place with a thousand bedrooms.

'I was in charge of the staff who cleaned the bedrooms and had to check that they'd done their jobs properly. It was a humbling experience. Many of them were refugees from places like Turkey and Afghanistan, older than me and very highly qualified, working in their home countries as doctors or engineers. I often ended up cleaning the rooms with them instead of just inspecting them afterwards.'

He nodded approvingly so I carried on explaining. 'I moved out of the housekeeping department and became a night auditor, a kind of accountant. I worked constant nightshifts for about a year.'

'So you'll not mind the shifts then,' he said.

'No, every job I've had since I left school has been shift work,' I replied. 'After a year of working nights I applied for a job for North West Airlines, an American company. I got the job and started working at Frankfurt Airport. Unfortunately I couldn't fly with them because I didn't have a green card.'

I was trying to work out what he would make of that. He smiled and nodded and I hoped he'd be more impressed with the kind of work experience I'd had than if I'd spent a couple of years on the checkout at the local supermarket. He seemed to be thawing a bit.

'Do you go to church?' he asked abruptly. The question took me by surprise, because I couldn't see what church attendance had to do with becoming a police officer and I wasn't sure what sort of answer was required.

'Well, my dad's a Catholic and he goes sometimes, but the rest of us don't. My mum's a Protestant. I believe in God but I'm not actually anything.'

At that point my mum came back into the room. I don't know if she'd been listening through the door and had decided that now would be a good time to intervene, but I was glad to see her.

'Do you want another drink, son?' she asked.

'Oh ay, I'll have another wee cuppa. How do you feel about Anne joining the police, Mrs Ramsay?'

My mum replied in her best posh accent again. 'I think it's a good job, son, lots of security, and I think Anne would make a great police officer. It's something she's always wanted to do.' She looked at him expectantly, hoping for a nod of approval that she'd said the right thing.

When she left the room again Inspector Robertson asked, 'And how does your brother feel about you joining the police?'

I knew that he would have checked out all the members of my family to see if any of them had a criminal record, as I'd been asked to put their names and dates of birth on my application form.

My lips felt suddenly dry and I decided that the best policy was to be honest and upfront. 'I don't really know how he feels about it but I imagine he's got his own opinion. My brother got into a bit of bother with the police because of his drug problems, but hopefully he can get himself sorted out. He's not a bad person,' I said.

Inspector Robertson nodded and made some notes, while I wondered if I'd said the right thing. I had a quick glance at the clock on the wall. He'd arrived just after 7 pm and it was now almost 8.30. I was surprised he had been here for such a long time and wondered how many more questions he had lined up for me. The next one threw me completely.

'What would you do if a married police officer came on to you?'

I looked him in the eye, wondering whether he was coming on to me himself or if he was asking a theoretical question. I decided it was the latter.

'I'd treat it the same way I would if anyone else came on to me and would deal with it as it happened,' I said.

He nodded and didn't pursue it.

'Righto then. That's it for now. I'll pass my report on to personnel and we'll be in touch soon.'

My mum emerged from the kitchen again. 'Thanks for your hospitality, Mrs Ramsay,' he said to her.

The first thing Mum said after she'd waved him off down the path and shut the front door was, 'Was I OK, was the house OK?'

She wasn't being self-centred but was very worried about the impression she had made. 'How did it go? I was trying to listen at the door,' she said.

'Alright,' I replied. 'He asked if we went to church!'

'What did you say?' my mum asked, looking slightly panicked in case I'd said the wrong thing.

'I just said Dad sometimes goes but that we didn't.'

'Should we be going to church?' she asked. 'Would that help you get in?'

'No, don't be daft,' I laughed, then added jokingly, 'I think he was coming on to me.'

'What d'you mean?' she asked horrified. 'Maybe you should think again about joining the police.'

'He asked me what I'd do if a married man came on to me!'

The doorbell rang again.

'Oh no, maybe he's forgotten something,' said my mum.

I opened the front door but it wasn't Inspector Robertson standing there, it was Eddie, one of the local drug-users, who had come to see if we wanted to buy any of the stuff he'd shoplifted that day.

'Any of you ladies looking for top-quality tights or some deodorant?' he said, adopting a tongue-in-cheek sales patter as he showed off the goods he'd just stolen from the local supermarket.

I laughed and said, 'Not today thanks.'

# Two

'Ouch,' I cried.

The tiny woman with the badly dyed auburn hair showed no mercy as she thrust the pin into my inner thigh. She was making the final alterations to the inside legs of my oversized police trousers.

'Stand still,' she barked. I decided that the best thing to do was to mind my manners. Eyeing her extra-large pin box, I kept my mouth shut and did as she said.

It had been a month since my home visit and I was happy and excited when I found out that I had been accepted. Now I was standing in what can only be described as a glorified cupboard on the third floor of Strathclyde Police headquarters getting fitted for my uniform. I felt like I was in an episode of the cartoon *Mr Benn*, stepping into a fantasy world and becoming a new character for the day. The room-cum-cupboard was packed with police uniforms in all shapes and sizes, but none of them seemed as manly as the one I was wearing.

'Right, get changed, that's you done,' said the flame-haired measurer. 'Just come out when you're ready and I'll go and get the rest of your uniform together.'

As I stood at the counter she reappeared armed with a tick list. 'Four shirts, two long-sleeved, two short, two trousers, two skirts, two tunics, three hats . . .'

Suddenly the phone rang, interrupting her in mid-flow. She answered quickly and I watched her screw her face up in disgust. I tried not to laugh as she snapped, 'I don't care if he's lost his gloves, he's not due another pair till next year.' The caller must have tried to persuade her. Not a chance. 'Too bad,' she smirked, slamming down the receiver and turning to me as if nothing had happened. Even though she was four inches shorter than me I found her scary.

'Two pairs of gloves, a handbag, four cravats, epaulettes, six pairs of tights, a raincoat, a fluorescent jacket.' She checked off each item before shoving them into a black polythene bin bag. I was surprised to see that we were given a handbag – I didn't realize policewomen carried one. It was medium-sized and made of cheap black vinyl with a silver zip and a thin shoulder strap. We were expected to carry our notebooks, pens, parking tickets and gloves in it.

'That's you till next year,' she said as she handed me the bag.

My first week in the police was at the local force training centre and was designed to break in the new recruits and prepare us for the following eight weeks at the Scottish police college, known as Tulliallan. The training centre was a huge pink building in the middle of Glasgow city centre and was referred to as the Pink Elephant.

I made friends easily with the other new recruits – fifteen

men and four more women – and got close to a girl called Julie. We were both twenty-one and had lots in common. She was taller than me, with long, dark hair and a huge smile, and was cheery and full of fun. We often spent our lunchtimes together heading over the Clyde Bridge to scan the rails of the local fashion shops.

Most of our instruction was done in classrooms.

'No hair below the collar for male officers, no loose strands of hair for females, all hair tucked under hats or locked in a hairnet, minimum make-up, stand up whenever anyone enters the room until you're told to sit down.'

We weren't given a choice about signing up to the Police Federation, St George's Welfare Fund and the Benevolent Fund. Money for our subscriptions was automatically taken out of our wages each month.

We were expected to salute when our uniforms were inspected, and the rank structure in the police was explained to us, along with the correct way to record information in our notebooks. We were given shoulder numbers that related to different divisions within Strathclyde Police. Mine was R274. I was told that R was Ayrshire. I stuck up my hand. 'Sergeant, Ayrshire's a bit far for me to travel. Could I not change to somewhere a bit closer?'

'You'll work where we tell you,' he retorted. 'When you signed up to become a police officer you automatically agreed to work anywhere that we decided in the Strathclyde area. You don't have a choice.'

I felt trapped and wondered what on earth I'd signed up for. It had never even entered my head that I might have to move far away from home, and I was dismayed that I had no choice in the matter.

I was sitting next to the only Asian recruit, a man called Ahmed Singh who was the only other officer going to R division out of our group. When the sergeant left the room Ahmed turned to me and said, 'I'm glad you asked that, I wanted to ask the same thing. I'm not happy about being sent to R division either, because there's no Asian community there. I think I'd be more useful in Glasgow where there are plenty of people from the same background as me.' I was in no doubt that however good any of our reasoning was, the decision had been made and that was that.

The day before we finished the week-long course they took us over to the Sheriff Court which stands across the road from the force training centre. They demonstrated how to fingerprint. Julie and I fingerprinted each other.

'God, I feel like a criminal,' she said when I fingerprinted her.

'You better watch it or you'll end up in one of the cells,' I joked. She laughed nervously.

Before we left the Sheriff Court the sergeant took all of our fingerprints and explained that they'd be kept on file. Alarm bells started to ring for me. Why on earth did they need our fingerprints when they'd already screened us to rule out criminal offences?

I asked the same sergeant I'd questioned about being sent to Ayrshire. 'Why do you need our fingerprints? Didn't you check us out already?'

He bridled at that. 'Everybody who joins the police has their fingerprints taken,' he said irritably. 'We only use them for crime scene comparisons, don't worry. We won't be giving them to anyone else.'

I wasn't convinced and didn't feel that he'd given me a straight answer, but I shut up because I could see I was getting on his nerves.

On the final day of our week of basic training Julie and I headed towards the force training centre shop to pick up the remaining items that we needed to go to Tulliallan.

As we went into the small shop I could see that the Strathclyde Police emblem was staring at me from every corner of the crammed room, painted or engraved on to mugs, badges, trophies and T-shirts.

'Who buys this crap?' I whispered to Julie.

We compared our lists and headed over to a pile of brown shoe boxes. I picked up one with 'size 5' written on the front and took out a pair of shiny black marching shoes to try on.

As I bent down to lace them up, Julie, who had already put her shoes on, started to tap-dance under my nose. I quickly got up to join in and we both fell about laughing.

'I cannae believe we're no supplied with these, ah grudge buying them,' I said.

'I'm no surprised they make you buy them, they couldnae give them away if they tried. They're ugly,' laughed Julie.

Still wearing the shoes, we slid across the carpet towards the swimsuits. We each picked one up in unison and held them against our bodies.

'Ah wouldnae be seen dead in this,' Julie said.

'Ma granny wouldnae be seen dead in it,' I laughed.

The ugly black costumes looked as though they had been designed for nuns, stretching from the neck down to the knees.

There was no getting out of wearing them because they were on our lists. I knew I'd never wear the swimsuit again after training.

'How do you think the first week went?' I asked Julie.

'It wisnae as bad as I thought, though I'm no very happy about getting posted to Oban, it's miles away,' she said. Oban is a fishing village ninety miles north-west of Glasgow.

'Ah know, I'm absolutely raging. I came home from Germany to be closer to my family but they're sending me to bloody south Ayrshire, forty miles away.'

Something else had been playing on my mind and I decided to confide in Julie. 'I've noticed that they weren't too happy about me asking so many questions,' I said.

'How do you know?'

'Well, I got pulled in by Chief Inspector Smith. He warned me that I wouldnae go very far if I asked so many questions. He said I was just to shut up and learn the job.'

'You're joking!' said Julie. 'Is that not what you're meant to do in this job?'

'I only asked him why female officers had to wear skirts rather than trousers, and he just said, "That's the way we do things here."'

Before I joined the police I'd been a real free spirit, loving nothing better than to set off for a new place on the spur of the moment with hardly a bean in my pocket. I lived life to the full and didn't have any worries. I never panicked about how I'd get by but always made the best of whatever situation I found myself in and readily made friends. In my teenage years I had collected pen friends from all over the world and was an avid letter-writer. My first week at the police training centre had left me feeling stamped on. I'd always been used to expressing my opinions freely, but that didn't seem to be welcome here. Still, I told myself that one week of training wasn't the real job. I wasn't the kind of person who gave up on things easily and I wanted to give my new career a proper chance.

The following week my dad drove me up to Tulliallan. It was about an hour's drive from Glasgow.

'Bloody traffic. It's murder at this time of day,' he grumbled.

'Sorry Dad, I really appreciate you driving me up.'

'It's OK hen, it's fine, we'll be there soon.'

We drove through a few picturesque villages and kept having to slow down to 30 miles an hour when the road narrowed, then we'd pick up speed again when it widened. The villages themselves only had a few hundred houses in them.

We drove in silence for a while. My dad seemed tense, as if he wanted to say something.

'Are you sure you want to do this job?' he asked finally.

'I want to give it a go. I really want to help people.'

'I understand that. You've always been that way. I remember the time when you stood up for Donna Brown when she was getting bullied at primary school. Her mother came up and thanked me at the parents' night. That made me so proud of you. Not everyone will speak up when they see that something's wrong.'

'I don't even remember that,' I said.

'I just hope this job isn't going to change you,' he said. 'I'm worried it's a bit dangerous, I don't want anything to happen to you.'

'Don't worry, Dad, I'll be fine. My other jobs haven't changed me and I'm sure this one won't either.'

When we crossed the Kincardine Bridge I knew we were getting close to the police college that was in the village of the same name. The college is the biggest thing in Kincardine and generates a lot of employment there.

We drove up the sweeping driveway of the picturesque castle of Tulliallan. It was set in lush green forest and looked impressive.

'It looks nice,' my dad said. 'But I'm still not happy about you doing this.'

'It looks great. Stop worrying, Dad, I'll be fine.'

This is where I would be spending my next eight weeks training with new recruits from all over Scotland. Alongside the original castle were newer buildings, including some cottages where scenarios that police recruits were likely to encounter were acted out.

I wheeled my suitcase across an area of open ground known as the parade square. In the distance I could see a large, imposing figure in full police uniform. A bright red sash covered his tunic and he was holding a stick. I couldn't see his features clearly but the red sash alone was enough to unnerve me. He was standing to attention staring straight ahead, his arms glued to his side. This place made me feel very small. It seemed to take for ever to cross the square towards the figure.

As I got closer I could see no trace of a smile on his hardened features. He appeared even bigger close up and the light reflected off his shaved head. Maybe Dad was right. For a moment I considered running back to the safety of his car.

I walked nervously past him through the double doors and

joined the army of eighty or so new recruits lined up in the foyer waiting for their names to be called.

The air was stiff with tension and you could hear a pin drop. There were more uniformed supervisors ahead of us, looking every bit as scary as the one outside.

Whitney Houston's powerful voice suddenly punctured the silence with the lyrics of 'I Will Always Love You'. I wondered where it was coming from and along with the others I started to giggle nervously, but stopped when I realized that the uniformed supervisors were not amused.

One of them approached the crowd. 'You, boy! Do you find that funny?' roared the inspector as he pointed his baton at one of the new recruits in front of me.

Whitney's voice continued to bellow out from the red-faced recruit's suitcase as he was led back out of the double doors.

His radio alarm clock had gone off by mistake and he was roundly told off. His card was marked.

I was directed to the female dormitory, which reminded me of a hospital ward. Army-style camp beds, a couple of dozen of them, lined both sides of the walls. I was allocated a bed at the far end of the room opposite a girl from Lothian and Borders police force who ignored my efforts to strike up a conversation. There was rivalry between the two biggest forces in Scotland – we Glaswegians versus the recruits from Edinburgh. We were seen as a bunch of ruffians while they considered themselves to be more refined.

The room quickly filled with female chat as we got to know each other. I found it interesting talking to some of the other girls and finding out if they knew things about the course that I didn't. But the chance to chat quickly came to an end as a female sergeant handed out our timetables. Work started almost at once.

Sergeant Farmer was one of the female sergeants acting as a supervisor. A few years older than us, she was an attractive woman but was quite bitchy towards the female recruits and seemed envious of the younger, prettier ones. She liked to be the centre of attention and often flirted with the young men on the course.

The days were full on, taken up with polishing shoes, pressing uniforms and trying to learn the law. There was no time to think and each night I fell into bed exhausted. We were constantly under pressure.

The sergeants who were our class instructors seemed to be on ego trips. They constantly drummed into us that we were now part of the biggest gang in the world.

As they took the classes, which covered everything from giving evidence and powers of arrest to questioning suspects and conducting searches of people or premises, they seemed intent on filling our heads with all the exciting crimes they'd been involved with. We stared wide-eyed with admiration and they lapped it up.

We had a lot of marching to do in our shiny black tap shoes. Strutting up and down made me feel really stupid and I wondered what it had to do with policing.

As well as us naive new recruits, the police college was also home to second-year trainees who seemed to be much more streetwise than us, traffic officers and seasoned officers on detective courses. The phrase 'the job's fucked' was a common line they used. I had no idea why.

One of the best things about the training was that I began

to lose a lot of weight as a result of the rigorous routine and the excessive exercise. Quite a few of the recruits were overweight and struggled with the forest runs, especially carrying tree trunks and running up hills. It was a nightmare running with a tree trunk with four handles on it, particularly if you were at the back. Some of the time I was running with three guys and felt as if I was getting dragged along. We did a lot of runs through the forest, and one of the things I hated most was repeatedly sprinting up Rice Crispie Hill (I never got to find out why it was called that) and jogging back down. Years later that particular exercise was abandoned because a new recruit sued the police after falling and breaking her ankle. We were expected to run a mile and a half in twelve minutes. We had to do as many pull-ups, sit-ups and press-ups as we could in two minutes. One of the police trainers tested us on this and gave us a grade according to how fit we were.

The main aim of the swimming classes was to learn life-saving skills. Male and female recruits were taught together. The men had to wear tight-fitting Speedos and we women all looked very unsexy in our droopy black swimsuits.

In one of the swimming classes we were asked to walk to the end of the diving board and then drop off it, keeping our bodies straight. Like a few of the other recruits I was scared to do this because I wasn't a good swimmer and the diving board was very high. Sergeant Miller, the PE instructor, tried everything to get me to do it but I refused point-blank. I was getting more and more scared. Each time I looked up at the diving board it seemed to have got higher. He appeared to have given up on me and started to walk away, but then he turned back and said, 'I think you're just a chicken.'

He had pressed the right button. I wasn't going to let anyone call me a chicken and get away with it. I marched straight past him, walked up the stairs and dropped myself off the diving board. The jump wasn't anywhere near as bad as I'd thought it would be and Sergeant Miller was delighted with me.

'Well done, Constable Ramsay. I knew you could do it.'

I smiled and grabbed my towel, pleased that I hadn't let my fears get the better of me.

One day after swimming we were told we were getting our photos taken immediately after we'd climbed out of the pool and dried ourselves.

I pulled my hair back and joined the other girls – we were all rushing around like a bunch of clucking hens trying to put on a bit of make-up. These were the photos that our mums would be proudly displaying on the mantelpiece and we all felt annoyed that they'd chosen this moment to take them.

'God, I look like shit, I wish they'd given us more time,' said one of the girls.

'Has anyone got any lip gloss?' asked another. We all looked like a bunch of drowned rats.

We were given stodgy food at mealtimes in the huge canteen. I'd noticed that a couple of the girls stuffed their faces with fatty food and then made a beeline for the toilets. When I went to the toilet I could hear them retching. They seemed to be unusually thin, but at the time I didn't realize that they were bulimic, not having encountered this illness before.

The guys who appeared ugly in week one all seemed godlike by week eight. It was because we were all going through such intense training that close relationships formed, both friendships and sexual liaisons. One of the married sergeants who was training us got together with one of the young female recruits during our time at Tulliallan and ended up leaving his wife for her. She later became pregnant by him.

One day we concentrated on role-playing exercises, with the class divided up into pairs to mirror the way we would be working on the street. There were five sergeants who played the roles of different criminals, such as a housebreaker, a man who'd urinated in the street and someone who'd caused a disturbance. We took it in turns to practise while the rest of the class watched and critiqued the performance. The scenario I was given was to stop a criminal and see if there were any warrants out for him. He was acting suspiciously and gave me a false name. The sergeant ended up telling me much more than he had planned to, testament to my skills at eliciting information. I got a pat on the back for that, but I was just being myself – I loved talking to people and asking them questions came naturally.

We were treated like children at Tulliallan and I resented that. Occasionally we were allowed to go for a drink in the evening in the police bar in the castle aptly named the Copper Lounge. But as with every part of our training we were watched closely by senior officers. A maximum of two drinks was permitted and we had to be in bed by a certain time. Judging by their bloodshot eyes and red-veined noses, the sergeants weren't bound by the same rules and drank heavily. I could hear raucous laughter from parties in their rooms well into the night.

We had the weekends off, and sometimes I travelled back to Glasgow with Julie. Often I didn't want to go back to

Tulliallan on Monday mornings, but I was determined to stick out the training.

At the end of the eight weeks I didn't feel that I knew a huge amount about policing, but one thing that had been drummed into me was that I must do as I was told at all times. The whole experience made me feel like a newly programmed robot. I was elated that I'd got through the course and hadn't been thrown out, relieved that my time at Tulliallan was over and eager to be assigned to a police station so that I could get cracking.

We had a passing-out parade that required us to march around the parade square to the sound of awful band music being played through loudspeakers. My parents and my sister Lynne came along. My mum was still keen to make a good impression with the senior officers and my dad still thought it was not the job for me, but he was proud I'd stuck out my training. Lynne found the marching and passing-out parade hilarious and decided to use the occasion to practise her film-making skills. She'd brought her video camera along to record the proceedings. My abiding memory of that day is of Lynne's head bobbing up and down in the crowd with a mischievous grin on her face, video camera on her shoulder, and the furry microphone brushing against the faces of the people in the audience.

# Three

Suddenly the door of the briefing room burst open and a mass of uniforms came surging towards me like a stampede of wild elephants. I sidestepped fast to avoid getting squashed. For all the notice the oncoming police officers paid to me I might as well have been invisible. They were a scruffy bunch and had just finished their shift. Ties were ripped off and radios were banged down before they spilled out of the back door in their civilian jackets. It was fifteen minutes before the start of my first ever shift – a night shift – at Greenhill police station. I'd arrived a few days before and had been given a poky room to stay in at the station. I would have much preferred to live at home, but I had no choice but to lodge in the police quarters because south Ayrshire was too far from Glasgow to commute.

The most important area of any police station is known as the uniform bar, which is divided into three parts. The back area is where prisoners are brought into the station for processing. This is known as the charge bar. The central area is where the duty officer, usually a sergeant, sits, along with a constable and civilian staff. In this area all the calls that come in are monitored, radios are handed in and out and prisoners' medical problems are listed on the walls. The keys to any locked areas are kept in a safe and need to be signed out. The production log for items seized from crime scenes is there, along with the lost property log and the road traffic accident book. The front office is where members of the public come in to report crimes or other incidents.

I was nervously hanging around the charge bar, an area in the police station where officers congregate, waiting to go into the briefing.

Greenhill police office is one of the bigger stations in the Strathclyde Police area. It's an ugly modern building with four floors. Unlike many of the divisional headquarters Greenhill has its own traffic division because there are so many serious road accidents in the area. There are lots of fast-moving roads which people use to get to south Ayrshire and from there on to a boat over to Ireland.

The top two floors of the police station were male and female single quarters accommodation used both during training courses held at the office and rented out to new recruits who had been posted far from home.

I stood out like a sore thumb in my freshly pressed uniform, although the late shift officers were obviously in too much of a hurry to notice me. The last of the constables approached the bar: he was young and walked with a swagger.

'You must be the Tim,' he said cockily as he placed his radio on the bar.

'Sorry?' I said taken aback. Tim is a derogatory word for a Catholic. I realized that because my first name was Bernadette he had wrongly assumed I was Catholic.

'My inspector was talking to me about the two new

recruits and said he was offered the Paki or the Tim. He told me he wasn't having any Catholic woman on his shift,' he said casually.

I was shocked by what he said, and by the easy way he said it. I couldn't believe that the police could be so bigoted and narrow-minded. 'I'm not even Catholic,' I said, and thought to myself, 'Thank God I'm not on his shift.'

'Wait till I tell him. My name's Jim by the way.'

'And I'm Anne. Nice to meet you.'

'Is this your first night?'

'Yes, I'm really nervous going out in the real world and all that. I forgot to lift my pen. Do you have a loan of one? I cannae see any lying around.'

'You'll be lucky. If you're no fast, you're last. They're like gold dust.'

'Really?' I said, surprised.

'Ah've only got the one,' he said, gripping his cheap biro as if it was made by Mont Blanc. 'But if it's just to write something down you can borrow it for a minute.'

'OK, thanks. I just want to fill out my notebook,' I said.

Reluctantly he handed it over. I noticed that he'd wrapped his police number round the end of it.

'That's a bit much,' I said, looking at the sticker on the pen.

'It's so I know it's mine,' he said. 'You better put your number on everything. My hat got stolen last week and it's a nightmare trying to get a new one.'

'But this is a police office.'

'It doesn't matter,' he laughed. 'Stuff gets stolen all the time.'

I raced upstairs to the fourth floor where my cramped, dingy bedroom was. It was always boiling hot and police sirens blared underneath me at all hours as emergency calls were answered. I tried not to cringe as I glanced up at the stained polystyrene ceiling tiles and down at the old-fashioned flowery carpet. The sparsely furnished room didn't look too different from one of the cells in the station. All of the other women's rooms were unoccupied and it felt a bit creepy alone on my floor. The new male recruits slept on the floor below.

I emptied out my bag and frantically searched for a pen. Finally I found one and wedged it firmly in the pocket of my scratchy police trousers. I grabbed a street map as well because I had no idea where anything was and raced back down-stairs. I felt the stiff outline of my warrant card in my pocket. Although the card stated that I was a police officer I couldn't quite believe it. I hadn't done anything yet.

As I walked down the corridor to the briefing room two older officers in suits walked past me and looked me up and down.

'Who's she?' I heard one say.

'I don't know but she's a bit of alright,' said the other.

I went bright red with embarrassment and had a horrible feeling they had turned to watch me walk away. I could sense their eyes locked on my bum.

The briefing room was empty, with cheap plastic chairs scattered randomly around. I sat timidly on one of them and looked at the walls, which were plastered with photos and photofits of suspected criminals. I shuddered. I was about to go out into the real world and face some real criminals. It was bad enough seeing their faces in photos. How would I feel

when I had to look them in the eye or take hold of their criminal wrists to lock them into handcuffs?

The other officers on the shift wandered in. There was only
one woman among them. A lot of them looked scruffy, and a
couple of them made obvious belching sounds. I had expected
to be working with officers who were a whole lot smarter,
leaner and, as far as their general demeanour was concerned,
more professional-looking.

'What a bunch of misfits,' I said to myself.

I had been watching the other officers so intently that I
hadn't realized everyone in the room was looking disapprov-
ingly at me.

'That's Dougie's chair,' one of the officers said accusingly
to me by way of introduction. I jumped up and found a chair
to sit on that didn't seem to belong to anyone. I was surprised
the officers didn't put their names on the chairs the way they
did with their cheap pens.

I was welcomed to the shift, and as I was introduced to
everyone I saw some of the officers wink at each other. Shoulder numbers were called out by the inspector who was in
charge of the briefing.

'R274 go with R783,' he said. R274 was my shoulder
number. I fixed my gaze on R783 – I wanted to make sure I
didn't let him out of my sight. He looked about forty and had
dark hair and a big handlebar moustache. Unlike most of the
officers, he was slim and wiry.

We were told to take out the police car referred to as
Romeo Alpha One.

One of the officers could see that I looked totally bewil-
dered. 'Don't worry, hen, the job's fucked,' he said. He talked

out of the side of his mouth and I saw that he had very few teeth. I didn't find much comfort in his words. I followed R283 like a sheep to the uniform bar and found out he was called Tony. He grabbed two radios and said, 'Move. We've got a call.'

We headed out into the back yard, jumped into the car and Tony accelerated hard.

'Where are we going?' I asked meekly.

'Up to Ailsa mental hospital. It's full of loonies and they keep wandering off. It's a real pain in the arse for us. Some nutter's gone missing and we need to take a report. Don't worry, I'll dae it, you watch.'

We drove in silence for the rest of the way until we reached the old asylum in the middle of some woods. Pictures flashed into my mind of *One Flew Over the Cuckoo's Nest.*

It was 11 pm and the place was in darkness. From the outside the hospital looked like an old country house. Tony pressed the intercom and we were buzzed in. The warden greeted us in the foyer. I thought he looked a bit cranky himself. The place seemed deserted, almost as if it was no longer being used as a hospital, although it had the telltale smell of disinfectant. I was keen to get out of there as soon as possible.

'Who is it this time?' asked Tony with a sigh.

'It's James Gardner,' said the warden.

'Ahh yes. I know James.'

Tony asked for details of when James had last been seen and what he was wearing.

'He didn't put his jacket on,' said the warden, 'so maybe he hasn't gone far this time.'

'No bother,' said Tony. 'We'll check the usual addresses, mind, and you let us know if he turns up.'

It was a freezing cold night and I was relieved to get away from the creepy hospital and back into the warmth of the car.

Tony picked up the radio and said, 'Romeo Alpha One.'

'Romeo Alpha One go ahead,' squeaked the voice of the controller.

'The missing person from Ailsa is James Gardner. He was last seen at 8 am by staff. We'll complete a missing person form.'

He relayed the details about James to the controller and a few minutes later a description of him went out over the radio. We were diverted to another call at the Sea Inn pub and other officers were sent to check various addresses where James had been found before.

We screeched to a halt outside the pub and ran in. It was a rundown, smelly and old-fashioned place, a typical working men's pub, its wooden floor sticky with spilt beer. Most of the drinkers were men with lived-in faces sitting with their half-pints of lager and their shorts of whisky.

There was a woman standing in the middle of the pub shouting. I guessed she was about fifty. Her hair a patchy peroxide blonde with black roots showing and she was dressed in tarty clothes more suited to someone half her age – a shiny black miniskirt and a low-cut bright pink top.

'Ya fuckin' bastard ye,' she said furiously to the landlord, realizing that he had dialled 999.

Like James Gardner this woman was someone Tony knew.

'Come on, Mary, calm down now,' he said as he approached her.

'Fuck off, you polis bastard,' she shouted at him.

I stood frozen to the spot. I had no idea what I was supposed to do and couldn't think of any useful contribution I could make. This was the first time that I was on show to the public as a police officer and it was an odd sensation. I was convinced that everyone was looking at me expecting me to take charge. I felt as if I was no longer Anne but had become the uniform. Any training I'd had went right out of the window.

Mary was strutting around like an ostrich. Tony grabbed one of her arms and signalled to me to take the other. Before I managed to do this, though, she lashed out at me, hitting me in the chest. Tony clipped a pair of handcuffs on to her skinny wrists and between us we managed to load her into the police car. She was steaming drunk, and I took a step back when the fumes on her breath hit my nostrils.

The landlord came out of the pub when Mary was safely in the back of the police car.

'You want a wee half for the road?' he asked Tony, who turned and looked at me.

'No, not now. Ah've got the bint with me,' he said under his breath. 'Maybe later.'

He told me to get into the back of the car with Mary. I slid into the back seat gingerly, trying hard to hide my nerves, and sat as far away from her as possible. She was still screaming and shouting and tried to spit in my face. 'Ah'm a witch, ah can see things,' she kept on saying.

When we arrived back at the police station we practically fell into the charge bar with Mary because she was struggling so much.

'Have you searched her yet?' asked the desk sergeant at the station. I shook my head and he handed me a pair of surgical gloves.

I tried to pat her down while Tony attempted to charge her. A group of police officers came up to see what all the commotion was about. With so many pairs of eyes trained on me I desperately hoped I wasn't doing the search wrong. I found a pack of tarot cards and a roll of Sellotape in her pocket – not the kind of things most people carried around.

One of the uniformed sergeants who also obviously knew Mary started winding her up. 'Will you read my cards, Mary?' he said. When she shook her head his tone grew harsher. 'Who've you been shagging on this cold night?'

As the other officers all laughed, another call came in over the radio.

'Romeo Alpha One, can you attend a housebreaker still on the premises at 5 Roman Road?'

Some of the other officers took over with Mary while Tony and I raced out of the door. As we drove towards the call he switched on the flashing blue light.

'Why haven't you put the siren on?' I asked innocently.

'Don't be stupid, hen. We don't want to let the housebreaker know we're coming.' Tony gave me a withering look and I cringed at my naivety.

He was driving at 60–70 miles an hour along dark, narrow

roads, bumping on and off pavements and overtaking everyone in his path. I sat rigid in my seat, terrified that he was going
to crash. Instinctively I kept putting my foot down on the floor
as if to brake.

Then the radio buzzed again: 'Romeo Alpha One, cancel,
cancel, FAGI, it was the householder the neighbour had spotted, not an intruder.'

'Why're we not going? What's a FAGI?' I asked Tony.

'False alarm, good intent,' he said. 'Some idiot neighbour
probably thought they were doing a good deed. Come on, let's
go for a coffee.'

My body sagged with relief that Tony was no longer driving like a maniac and putting our lives in danger. Even better,
we didn't need to go to a house where I imagined some crazed
man armed with a knife was waiting to pounce on us.

We sat sipping coffee from polystyrene cups bought from
a mobile burger van, the heat from the drinks steaming up the
windscreen.

'So how long have you been in the police force?' I asked,
desperate to make conversation. Before he could answer
another call came over the radio for us. A sheep had wandered
on to the motorway and wouldn't budge.

'Surely they should be calling the farmer not the police for
something like that,' I thought. Tony explained that because
traffic travelled so fast the sheep could cause an accident and
motorists had to be warned about its presence.

We parked the car on the road with the blue light flashing.

'I never thought I'd be doing this kind of thing when I
joined the police,' I said to Tony.

'I know. It's a load of shit,' he admitted, 'but we have to do it.'

Twenty minutes later another police car came to relieve us and we headed back to the station to take our break. It was 4 am and I was exhausted. I sank into one of the squashy chairs in the station lounge and nodded off.

Twenty minutes later Tony's voice jolted me awake. 'Come on, hen, we need to go to the hospital,' he said, buttoning up his tunic. I hadn't even heard the call come in over the radio. I jumped to attention and fastened up my cravat.

As we drove to the hospital Tony asked casually, 'Ever seen a dead body before?'

I shook my head and once again I froze, my imagination running riot. I was panicking, but Tony mustn't see how scared I was. I followed him dutifully into the hospital praying that another call would come through that would take us away from dead bodies.

We had to walk down four flights of stairs into the basement. Every step felt like the death march as I followed Tony through double steel doors into the freezing cold mortuary. There were lots of fridges with body-sized pull-out drawers, and on a mortuary slab in the middle of the room a body lay.

A porter was waiting for us and signalled that the body on the slab was the one we had to deal with.

'I'll leave youz to it,' he said. He looked relieved to be able to leave and scurried off.

The body was white and bloated, as if someone had inflated it, and to my horror it had no eyes. I somehow managed to stop myself from screaming. I wanted to run back up the four flights of stairs, hand my police uniform back and say, 'It was all a terrible mistake, I don't want to be a police officer after all.'

Instead I stepped back and shivered. I didn't want to get too close to the body. Tony walked closer and had a good look at it. 'I need to go and get some bags,' he said. 'You wait here.'

Once again my heart sank. The last thing on earth I wanted to do was wait there, by myself, with a swollen corpse. I longed to be tucked up in bed surrounded by the living. Most of the room was in semi-darkness, but some recessed lights cast a ghostly half-light over the body. I stood in the shadows, desperately trying to stop myself from shaking. I wondered what had happened to the eyes and was convinced that at any moment the body was going to jump up and attack me the way they do in trashy horror films. My imagination was running riot now. Maybe by the time Tony returned with the bags it would be me laid out eyeless on the slab. But I wasn't ready to die. I dared myself to look again at the body just in case it was moving. It lay absolutely still. The skin had a waxy pallor and I could see a bluish tinge under it. I edged towards the door.

Tony reappeared carrying polythene bags. Just when I thought things couldn't get any worse he told me, 'We need to strip him.'

For a minute I thought he was joking.

He glanced at me and could see that my colour was almost as bad as the corpse's. He began cutting the clothes off and didn't push me to help him. I was shocked to see just how bloated the whole body was. Tony asked me to tie a label on to the toe. My hands were shaking as I tried to tie it on without actually touching the body.

'OK, let's go now,' said Tony. I never thought those four words would bring me such joy.

We climbed back up the stairs and once we got back to ground level Tony turned his radio on and spoke to the controller.

'James Gardner's turned up,' he said.

# Four

'What do you fantasize about?' he asked. It was 6 am on my first early shift. I was half-asleep and sitting in the police car with an officer called Frank who I'd never worked with before. I hadn't seen that coming but quickly knocked it on the head.

'A big roll and bacon,' I said firmly. That shut him up. We drove on in silence. I leaned back and closed my eyes. I'd completed my first set of seven night shifts, then had three days off, and now I was starting my first set of seven early shifts.

I couldn't get James Gardner out of my mind. After leaving the mortuary and finishing that first shift I'd breathed a huge sigh of relief. Tony and I had finished late and the rest of the officers had already gone home by the time I handed my radio back in at the police station. I'd crawled straight into bed and had spent the next few hours tossing and turning in my overheated bedroom in the police station. Tony had said to me at the end of the shift, 'You did well, hen,' but I couldn't relax. I was feeling wired, I had nobody to talk to about what I'd just seen, and I couldn't imagine ever getting used to dealing with this kind of thing. Eventually I fell into a fitful sleep.

Thankfully the next few nights were less eventful, although

every single day just as I was dropping off to sleep around 7.30 am I was jolted awake by the sound of police sirens.

The radio interrupted my thoughts, telling us about a suspected theft at a residential home for adults with learning disabilities like Down's syndrome. As we walked into reception I saw that Frank was giving the pretty receptionist the same leering look he'd given me when he found out I was his partner for the day. She was very young and looked uncomfortable. I felt embarrassed too because I was representing the police and had to watch Frank undressing the poor girl with his eyes.

'We're looking for Mr Jones,' I said, in the hope of reminding Frank why we were here.

I could see several adults with Down's syndrome sitting chatting in the lounge. A man appeared and introduced himself as Mr Jones.

'We've had information that one of our residents, a man called William McDonald, has stolen a benefits book belonging to another resident,' he told us. 'He's a small-time, petty thief but he managed to con the court into thinking he was a bit daft and they sent him here.'

He took us to William's room so that we could search it. William was a small man with a pinched face and didn't have the features of someone with Down's syndrome. He nodded when we asked for permission to do a search. A strange stench hit my nostrils; it was a bit like the odour of a dead animal. My eye was drawn to pictures of girls with Down's syndrome plastered all over his wall. Frank searched one side of the room while I searched the other. I was terrified of what I was going to find and I knew it was likely to be something far more sinister than a benefits book.

I turned back the sheets of William's bed and saw bloodstains. Panic rose up into my throat. I knelt down and searched under the single bed, which was pushed against the wall. The stench was getting stronger. I kept looking over at Frank and he at me. An image of James Gardner's eyeless corpse flashed into my head. There was more blood on the carpet under the bed and what looked like a bloodstained towel in a dark corner against a wall. I pulled the bed out to get a closer look and then I discovered the source of the smell and the blood.

Used sanitary towels and tampons were piled under the bed, mounds of them. I opened a bedside drawer and found more. Frank discovered others stashed elsewhere in the room. They were everywhere. This was one scenario we hadn't prepared for at Tulliallan!

'What are you doing with all these tampons?' Frank asked William. His tone was calm and even, as if he was questioning him about the benefits book he had expected to find rather than the bloodied sanitary towels that he certainly hadn't.

William shrugged, as if collecting used sanitary products was as normal as collecting stamps.

'Sometimes I take them out of bins and sometimes I take my girlfriend's,' he explained nonchalantly. We didn't find the stolen benefits book, and as it isn't a crime to store used sanitary towels there was nothing else to do but leave.

I had been so shocked I couldn't speak in William's room, but once I got back into the car with Frank I told him how sick I thought the whole thing was.

Frank, however, seemed completely unperturbed by what

we'd found. 'That's nothing. You should have seen the guy I came across last week. We were searching his house and he wouldn't let us touch a bucket that looked as if it had wall-paper paste in it. In the end he broke down and told us he'd been wanking into the bucket for the last year.'

'Oh . . . my . . . God,' I said, horrified. I had no idea that I'd be dealing with such bizarre incidents when I joined the police. 'What did you do with it?'

'We emptied it out in case there was anything in it.'

I managed a nervous laughed.

'You'll get used to it, doll. You'll see it all in this job. Nothing surprises me any more.'

I couldn't imagine ever getting used to things like that.

Each police station had four groups of officers working out of it. There were three shifts in a twenty-four-hour period. One group of officers worked on each shift while the fourth had time off. Officers remained in the same group and rotated between early, late and night shifts and time off. Over the next few months I got paired up with most of the officers in my group. It was a very steep learning curve because they all had such different personalities. One night I was with Stewart, a broad man of twenty-seven, six foot five inches tall with hands like shovels. He'd recently become a father for the first time. He talked non-stop about his baby and was always exhausted.

We drove slowly up a busy dual carriageway near to the police office. As we came to a set of red lights a BMW in the lane next to us took off at speed. Stewart suddenly roused himself from his torpor and hit the blue lights and the klaxons as he accelerated after the car. He told me to radio in for assistance. Adrenalin had kicked in and my heart was racing. I imagined all kinds of dramatic crimes – a dead body in the car, a mad axe killer, a Colombian drug baron. The car was weaving between lanes of traffic and we were right on its tail doing the same thing. After a minute or two I realized with horror that I couldn't see the back of a driver's head in the driving seat – the car seemed to be driving itself.

'That's fucking weird. Who the hell's driving that car?' said Stewart.

I wondered if it was being powered by remote control. The car carried on speeding then slowed and suddenly spluttered to a halt as if it had run out of petrol.

We both jumped out of the patrol car. My heart was beating faster than ever as we ran to the driver's window. I was bracing myself to deal with a violent man. The last thing I expected to see was a wee cherubic face peering up at us through the window. I gazed, bemused, at a beautiful small boy with angelic blue eyes and blond hair. I guessed he wasn't more than nine or ten years old and his head barely reached the steering wheel. He smiled at us, slowly raised himself up, pointed two fingers at us, then locked the doors from the inside.

'Open the fucking door ye wee bastard,' shouted Stewart. 'Oh it's Jamie Rodgers, up to his old tricks. He's the only ten-year-old who knows how to drive a car round here. I should have known.'

Stewart picked up his baton, smashed the driver's window smartly, removed the remaining bits of glass, reached in, grabbed Jamie and pulled him out through the window. The angelic boy was now kicking and flailing his arms. 'Fuck off pigs,' he screamed.

He looked tiny in Stewart's huge hands. A report describing Jamie's theft of the car was sent to the children's reporter, a panel of experts in child welfare, but not much could be done because Jamie was a juvenile. He knew that until he got a bit older the police couldn't touch him, and according to Stewart he was an expert at playing the system.

Most of the things I had to deal with during my probation were breaches of the peace, one of the most common crimes committed. This offence covers anything from someone shouting and swearing in the street, to taking part in a stand-up fight or being a peeping Tom. Most of my night shifts were spent sitting outside one of the three nightclubs in Greenhill town centre waiting for the revellers to spill out. I kept my eyes peeled for drunken brawls whilst most of the male officers were more interested in chatting up the inebriated, scantily clad young women.

A few weeks later I was paired up with an officer called Gerry for my shift.

Dougie, the officer whose chair I had innocently sat on at my first briefing, came up to us and said, 'Hope y'are no gone be shagging aboot the night, Gerry.'

Gerry laughed. 'Shut up you fat bastard.'

We were going out in the van Romeo Mike 3. I noticed it had a mattress in the back.

'What's that for?' I asked.

'Ahh, that's for the ladies,' said Gerry grinning. I couldn't tell if he was joking or being deadly serious. As soon as he had turned the key in the ignition he started to reel off a whole catalogue of sexual antics that he got up to on his shifts.

Once again I wasn't sure if he was just bragging or if he really did manage to copulate with half the women of Greenhill while he was on patrol.

'There was one lassie, big Myra, she had great big jugs and she was bouncing up and down topless on my knee wearing my police hat, while I was driving the patrol car. I had my blue light on and everything.'

I couldn't think of any kind of a suitable response to that and decided it was best to say nothing.

We drove to a local baker's, who came out and handed Gerry a huge bag of rolls and some extra plastic bags. I noticed that he didn't pay for them and wondered why. Then we drove to a newsagent's and this time the same thing happened with a handful of newspapers. Once again Gerry didn't hand any money over. He and the newsagent both behaved as if this was completely routine, but I didn't have a clue what was going on. Last stop was the fish van. Gerry got out and came back with a few pieces of fish wrapped up in paper. I assumed that once again no money had changed hands. We drove to a quiet spot and he started parcelling the items up into separate plastic bags.

'Are they for the station?' I asked.

'Naw hen, they're for my birds. They wake up in the morning, get Gerry's parcels and think I'm a great guy.'

By the time he'd finished explaining he'd wrapped up five mixed packages of bread, fish and newspapers. We drove round leaving them on various doorsteps. Gerry ignored the calls coming in over the car radio – this was much more important. I was gobsmacked.

When he'd finished he switched his own radio back on and

took a call to help a woman who had been locked out of her house in a posh part of town. She was in her mid-forties, small and slim with mousy brown hair.

Gerry sauntered up to her, looked her boldly in the eye and grinned. She immediately began fiddling self-consciously with her hair.

'I've been locked out,' she said coyly.

'Don't worry, we'll get you in,' he told her. He put his arm round her shoulder and gave her a quick squeeze.

'Ooh, ah've not had a cuddle for more than three years,' she said, giggling.

'Well ah'm yer man,' Gerry replied with a glint in his eye. I wanted to reach for the sick bag but the woman obviously had no problem with Gerry's clichéd patter.

'There's a small window open up there, maybe I could squeeze through that,' she said to him. Gerry nodded and helped lift her up so she could climb through the window. He had both his hands on her bottom and he turned and gave me a quick wink.

She managed to get into the house and then opened the front door. Gerry turned to me and said, 'Go and check out her car, hen, find out if it's registered to a man. Did you clock if she was wearing a wedding ring?'

I said drily that I hadn't noticed. Gerry disappeared into the house. I read her car number plate over the radio so that a Police National Computer check could be done on it. I knew it wasn't the right use of the computer but I wanted to fit into my new job so I did as I was told.

As the minutes ticked by I thought to myself, 'He can talk the hind legs off a donkey.'

I wished he would hurry up. I picked up the newspaper off the back seat and started reading. Every few minutes the radio blared into life.

The voice on the radio appealed for officers to attend calls to a house alarm going off, a disturbance at the race course and a road traffic accident. I ignored them all. Without Gerry I wasn't in a position to take any action. I was getting cold and bored but I tried to distract myself by doing the crossword. Each time the radio blared I felt twitchy. I assumed Gerry was giving the woman crime prevention advice, but how long could it take to talk about window locks?

It was almost an hour later and I'd long since finished the paper when he finally emerged. He had a big grin on his face like the cat who'd got the cream. Shutting the front door behind him, he casually zipped up his flies.

# Five

I was sitting on the floor in my mum's lounge, balancing the telephone between my neck and shoulder whilst trying to paint my toenails.

'So what time are we meeting up?' I asked Clare, one of the female recruits I'd joined with.

'Well Julie's coming to my house to get ready and my husband's going to drop us off at the pub. Probably about seven thirty,' she replied.

'No bother,' I said. 'I'll see you in there.'

I was excited to be seeing the girls I'd trained with at Tulliallan. We'd all been so busy working different shifts in different towns that this was the first chance we'd had to meet up in Glasgow. I couldn't believe almost a year had passed since I joined the police.

With my toenails still drying I hobbled into the kitchen. 'Mum, do you know where that purple top of Lynne's is?'

'She's just bought it. She'll kill you,' Mum said.

'What she doesn't know won't hurt her,' I said, and ran upstairs to look for it.

When I was ready to go I glanced at myself in the hall

mirror one last time before turning and kissing Mum on the cheek.

'You watch yourself and call me if you're going to be late,' she said.

'Mum, for God's sake, I'm going on a police night out, I think I'll be quite safe!' I laughed.

The pub we were meeting at was a well-known police haunt, but oddly enough it also attracted local criminals. It was a busy, city-centre establishment that served cheap drinks and so drew in people from all walks of life. Cheesy pop music blasted out, the air was thick with smoke and the heating was on to encourage people to drink more.

Off-duty police officers, mostly men, stood together in little huddles. It didn't matter that they wore their own clothes; their arrogant poses and swagger singled them out. Their voices drowned out the pub music as they boasted of their conquests. I noticed that some of them were giving each other the funny handshakes that I'd come to recognize as Masonic greetings. Although I didn't know any of them they looked very similar to the guys from the shift I worked on.

'Anne, Anne!' I could hear Julie's voice calling out to me through the crowd and saw her waving frantically from the corner of the bar. Feeling relieved, I headed towards her but struggled to reach her because the bar was so busy.

'What are you drinking?' she shouted over to me. 'We've started a kitty. Clare's sitting over there.' She pointed to a table by the window. I gave her my drink order and fought my way back through the crowd to where Clare was sitting.

Clare and I gave each other a big hug. She was a few years older than me and had married young before she joined the police. Unlike Julie and me, who were both tall and slim, she was small and plump and was also the most sensible out of the three of us.

'This is Paul, my partner from work,' said Clare, turning towards a guy who was sitting beside her.

'Pleased to meet you Paul,' I said smiling.

At that moment Julie appeared with a tray of drinks and placed them on the table. 'It's so good to see you, Anne,' she said hugging me. 'What have you been up to?'

'Oh God, I don't even know where to start,' I said. 'It's been crazy, nothing like I expected. Yesterday I was Princess Anne's toilet attendant. She was visiting the racecourse. I had to stand in a toilet for two hours just in case she needed a pee. She didn't. And on my very first shift I saw a dead body. It was horrible and had no eyes.'

They both looked shocked and wanted to know more.

'He was a missing person, just a young guy. He'd committed suicide by throwing himself into the sea. The cop I was working with told me that when a body is in the water for a long time the sea creatures eat into the orifices. And sometimes the limbs come away when you try to pull it out of the water.'

'Ew, that's horrible,' said Clare.

'It gets worse,' I told her. 'We had to strip the body but I couldn't bear to touch him.'

'I couldn't cope with that. We don't need to strip the bodies in Glasgow; the mortuary attendants do it for you,' said Clare.

'You're lucky, we need to strip them in Oban,' said Julie. 'I had a suicide too, it was awful. A sixteen-year-old girl who hanged herself from the loft in her house and was discovered by her three-year-old niece.'

'God, how did you handle that?' I asked.

'I don't know how I got through it. The family were in bits. It was all over a boy. She left a suicide note saying her boy-friend had kissed another girl. How sad is that.'

'I've seen a hanging too,' said Clare. 'Was her tongue black?'

'Ay, ah think that's normal with hanging. Listen to me talk-ing as if it's just matter-of-fact,' Julie said.

'Do you think you'll ever get used to the dead bodies?' I said. 'Because I'm finding it really hard to cope with. I keep getting flashbacks.'

'I'd rather just not talk about it,' said Clare. 'Let's have some fun instead for a change!'

Clare's colleague Paul had left the table – now he returned carrying a tray of drinks.

'Doubles, ladies,' he said, placing the tray down.

'Thanks Paul, you're a honey,' said Clare. Paul left and rejoined his friends at the bar.

'Cheers!' we said, raising our glasses. 'The job's fucked,' added Julie. We all laughed. I glanced at the police who were standing by the bar. They all seemed to be downing glass after glass of shorts.

'I can't believe how much the police drink,' I whispered to Julie. 'I'm not used to drinking so much, I don't think I'll be able to keep up.'

'Ah'm not a big drinker either,' she whispered back. 'I don't know how they manage to get into work the next day drink-ing the amount they do.'

'Paul seems like a nice guy,' I said, turning to Clare.

'He is, I've been dead lucky. He's been my partner since I started.'

'He's no bad-looking,' said Julie. 'Is he married?'

'Ay, unfortunately, with two kids,' replied Clare.

'You behave yourself, Clare; you're married too,' said Julie.

'There's nothing wrong with looking,' Clare replied flippantly.

'I've been told I'm getting a permanent partner,' I chipped in. 'He's called Gary and I've worked with him once before. He's a really good cop, not a sleazeball thank God.'

'Speaking of sleazy, wait till you hear what happened to me,' said Julie. 'A guy on my shift turned up at my house to show me his puppies.'.

Clare and I burst out laughing.

'He was trying to give me one,' said Julie.

'I bet he was,' I said, laughing louder.

'Did you let him?' Clare asked cheekily.

'Naw,' said Julie. 'But I nearly gave him one with my right foot right in the short and curlies.'

We all fell about laughing. When we managed to compose ourselves Clare said, 'By the way, I heard Ahmed Singh left. Was he not posted to Greenhill with you, Anne?'

'Ay, he was on a different shift from me. Between you and me it was more to do with race and religion. I heard he was getting a really hard time from his shift inspector. The same inspector who thought I was Catholic because of my name. He thinks that all women are bints,' I said.

'I hate that word,' said Clare. 'Mind you, the policewomen

in my office get called split arses or torn arses, which is even worse.'

'Have you heard of bikes or dykes?' asked Julie.

'What does that mean?' I asked.

'Duh! That policewomen are either sluts or lesbians,' Julie replied.

Paul reappeared at our table with two of his shift pals and yet another tray of drinks.

'Are you no gonna introduce us to your pals, Clare?' asked one of the guys. Without giving her the chance to speak he held his hand out to Julie and me and said, 'Hi, I'm John and this is Mark.'

They were both in their thirties and seemed like a pair of chancers. I noticed that both of them were wearing thick wedding bands.

'So how do you know Clare?' John asked me.

'We joined the police together,' I answered.

'No way, you're too good-looking to be a policewoman.'

'That old one,' I thought. I'd heard it a million times already and wondered if these guys learnt their cheesy lines out of the same secret manual. John didn't take the hint easily and continued to bombard me with more cringeworthy chat-ups.

I turned my back on him and started talking to Julie, who was obviously having the same problem with Mark. It seemed to do the trick and they moved away towards another group of women. ·

Clare stood up. 'I'll go and get another round in.' Her speech was slurred and she was slightly worse for wear.

'Don't bother, we've still got one and I need to go soon,'

said Julie. Clare ignored us and headed off to the bar with Paul.

'Ah hope that's no your police issue tights you're wearing,' I said to Julie, laughing.

'Aye it is, you couldnae ask for better protection. They should make condoms out of these,' she grinned.

'Ah know, I fell wearing mine. My leg was in a right mess but there wisnae a mark on the tights,' I said. 'They're bloody bullet-proof.'

'God, ah feel quite pissed,' said Julie.

'No wonder. That guy Paul's been buying us doubles all night,' I said.

'I cannae drink any more, I really need to go, I'm on early shift.' Julie was reaching for her jacket. 'It's been really great seeing you, Anne. Are you coping OK?' she asked

'I don't know, I'm still just trying to learn the job. I like helping people but it's not like I thought it would be, it's been a real eye-opener.'

'At least we've got each other,' she replied and gave me a hug.

As I hugged Julie back my eyes were drawn to the corner of the bar. Julie turned around to see what I was looking at.

Clare and Paul were standing close together, almost touching, gazing deeply into each others eyes.

# Six

As my partner Gary and I drove along the coastal road, I was sure that few police officers had a more beautiful beat to cover, surrounded by lush green hills on one side and a clear blue shimmering sea on the other. We were on the west coast, about an hour away from Glasgow, and a lot of the crimes we had to deal with involved sheep and other countryside matters. Greenhill itself is near the sea, surrounded by former mining villages with the stunning coastline close by. On a clear day you can see across the water to Ireland. The south is quite posh but the north is rougher with more council estates. A short drive away there is a holiday camp by the sea where we were often called to break-ins and drunken brawls.

Gary and I had been working together for a couple of months. He was a tall quiet man with blond hair which he wore in a side parting, bright blue eyes and cheeks that were ruddy from the fresh air rather than too much drink. I quickly realized that I had struck lucky when I was paired up with him. He was thirty-nine and had been in the force for about eighteen years. He was happily married and had three grown-up children. He adored them all and often chatted to me about what they were doing. I felt very comfortable talking to him about my family in Glasgow and I could tell him openly when I was missing them more than usual.

Everything about Gary was quiet, steady and reassuring. He didn't join in with the big boozy police nights out, which I felt was a real point in his favour, and he didn't feel the need to chatter about nothing in particular. If neither of us had anything to say we drove in companionable silence. Sometimes we sat in the patrol car eating ice creams and often we shared sandwiches. I was quite mature for my age, probably because I'd lived abroad for a while, and he recognized and respected that in me. In turn I respected his quiet professionalism and the way he encouraged me and tried his best to boost my confidence when I did something for the first time.

'Don't worry, nobody knows the job at the beginning. You've got plenty of common sense and you're a fast learner,' he often said to me if I expressed doubts about my ability to handle a particular incident. I learnt a lot from him. I watched the way he didn't steam into any incident we were called to, passing instant judgement on what had happened and who had done what. Instead he stood back appraising the situation before deciding what to do next. I tried to do the same.

House break-ins, drunken assaults and shoplifting were the kind of things I dealt with regularly. I'd been in the police for a year now and was becoming more confident in my work. I was starting to take charge when it came to asking people questions instead of just watching other officers ask. I realized that once I'd dealt with a certain crime I knew the right way to approach similar crimes when they happened.

Break-ins were particularly common, in both commercial

and residential properties. If the suspected housebreaker was still on the premises we had to call in a dog-handler. We sent the dog in before the officers to sniff out where the person was hiding, because the dog would find them faster than we would. Sometimes – not often, thankfully – the housebreaker would stab the dog with a screwdriver or other weapon to try and escape.

The drunken assaults could be anything from a stand-up fight to hitting someone over the head with a bottle, or a wife stabbing her husband accidentally. Alcohol caused a lot of crime, particularly amongst young people, that wouldn't have happened if they hadn't been drinking. Sometimes I had to take people straight to hospital, now and again getting spattered with their blood en route. You can't talk to somebody who's drunk and aggressive and I learnt that the best thing to do was to try and defuse tension. If people became violent another officer and I had to restrain them.

I found dead bodies less shocking than I had done when I first joined the police, and was able to develop a professional detachment because I hadn't known them as living, breathing people. But delivering death messages to often unsuspecting relatives was another matter. I was sure that however many times I did it I would never get used to it. It was dreadful to witness the raw shock, disbelief and hysteria that took hold of people when I broke the news that their loved one had died suddenly. I was never sure how long to stay and comfort them for, and knew that even the most carefully chosen words of sympathy could not reach them in the dark place they found themselves in after they heard the news. We didn't receive any training in how to break bad news, although no amount of training could really soften such a blow.

Nobody liked having to break distressing news, and many officers dealt with the ordeal using black humour back at the station. 'Are you the widow Smith?' was the grim joke bandied around about how to break bad news to an unsuspecting wife. At the beginning of January every year a bet was made between the divisions over where the first murder of that year would be.

When someone had died in particularly grievous circumstances I did my best to shield their relatives from the most graphic details. One middle-aged man had died in a house fire. I had never before seen a human body transformed into such a horrific sight. He was completely black and charred and the acrid smell of burning flesh rushed into my nostrils when I looked at him. His clothes had melted into his skin, which was ripped and blistered and exploding with lesions. He seemed to have fallen asleep lying on his side before the blaze started, because half of his face was burnt but the other half had more or less escaped the flames.

After the fire crews pulled his body out of his bedsit and an ambulance transported it to hospital, Gary and I had to follow the ambulance in a police car. A woman believed to be the dead man's daughter was traced, and came sobbing to the hospital to identify her father. She stood in another room and gazed sorrowfully at him through a large partition window. We didn't want her to get too close to that smell, or to reach out and turn back the sheet.

Gary had asked me to 'window-dress' the body – in this case to drape the sheet that was covering the man's body over the burnt half of his face in the hope that she would be able to identify him from the unburnt side without seeing just how horrifically charred he was. Even with so much of his body covered, she could see that the man was her father. She clapped a hand over her mouth in horror and nodded briefly when I said quietly, 'Is that your dad?'

'Can I see him?' she asked between sobs.

'I don't think that's a good idea,' I said, leading her gently away. I felt devastated for her, and shuddered when I thought about how I'd feel if it was my dad lying there in that state.

Another job I loathed, although it was much less traumatic than delivering death messages, was acting as turnkey to female prisoners held in police cells. Because there were so few female officers I was often called on to give female prisoners their meals and to deal with other issues. I was normally called in mid-shift, something I got annoyed about, because it stopped me from remaining on the street to deal with crime. The work was tedious and often I would chat to the women to pass the time.

'What are you in for?' was a common question. Usually the women's crimes were minor, but one day a very ordinary-looking woman caught me off guard when I asked her.

'Murder.'

I looked at her in amazement. I don't know what female murderers are supposed to look like but I was sure it wasn't like her – a young woman like myself.

Her story was a bizarre one. She lived in a smart part of Greenhill with her sister and a man who was sleeping with both women. All three were members of the street's Neighbourhood Watch scheme, so they knew when anyone was going away on holiday. Two elderly sisters and a brother lived in the street and told their neighbours of their plans to go away to Blackpool for a weekend. The brother ran a bookmaker's, and the man decided he would break into their home, steal the keys to the bookmaker's and grab the takings. What he didn't know was that one of the elderly sisters took ill at the last minute and decided to stay at home.

He broke into the house as planned, and brought with him the two women in his life. Once inside, they discovered to their horror that the elderly woman was at home. She'd been in bed, got up because she heard a noise and disturbed them whilst they were searching upstairs.

The man beat her up, and finally hurled her down the stairs to her death with the help of the two sisters. He snatched the keys and stole the money from the bookmaker's but was later found out when one of the two sisters he was living with came forward and told the police what had happened. Their house was searched, and as well as money from the bookmaker's the police found that it was full of stolen property from a spate of housebreakings that had recently been carried out in that area.

The woman told me everything in a very matter-of-fact way.

As I took her empty food tray from her I felt convinced that the fact that she slept with the same man as her sister and even made herself an accomplice to murder showed how thoroughly she was being manipulated by her lover.

Sometimes I felt that every possible combination of human misery was wrapped up in police work. One of the most appalling accidents I came across in all my years in the job happened on a fast country road. A boy was hit and killed by a car as he tried to cross the road to his home. He was with his brother, who went racing into the house to tell his mother what had happened. Blinded by grief, she rushed out to see to her child, and as she ran across the road towards him she too was hit by a car and killed. Gary and me arrived on the scene after both deaths and were glad to be assigned to diverting the traffic rather than have to deal with the bodies or the surviving son.

Although people generally call the police when something bad has happened rather than anything good, most of the things I came across were thankfully not as grim as that charred body or the double road death. Some of the incidents we were called out to were very minor and even light-hearted. In Greenhill we still got called out to rescue cats up trees, something I found hilarious. These call-outs tended to come from a posh part of town, where to the residents having their cat stuck up a tree was a serious matter.

I never ventured up to rescue Tiddles, and instead said pointedly that this wasn't really a police matter. On a few occasions when I made this remark the residents mentioned the name of a senior police officer they were friendly with and threatened to complain to him if I didn't start climbing straight away. I stuck to my guns though, and my feet stayed firmly planted on the ground.

I learnt a lot about policing and even more about human nature in the course of my day-to-day work. I loved the sheer variety of people and situations we encountered – the job was rarely boring.

One morning a few months into my placement Gary and I

were driving along in the car heading towards New Cumnock, squabbling over what music to put on the radio. It was outside our normal boundary but we'd been sent there to work for the day. As he was driving he kept trying to change the radio to the rock channel and I kept slapping his hand away. I was more in the mood for easy listening.

'Leave it alone, we're always listening to rock music,' I said.

'That's the only kind of music I like.'

'Well it might not be by the end of the day.'

We parked up in a huge field, and even before we got out of the car we could hear the thumping bass line of rave music. I could see there was another field which already seemed to be chock-a-block with ravers. A farmer had given permission for it to be used for a fourteen-hour rave and there were going to be bands playing all night. We were just two of the hundreds of officers drafted in to keep the peace. I stuck with Gary. I didn't really know what I was doing, but he'd obviously been to a few of these events before.

'Don't worry, it'll probably be quite peaceful,' he said. 'They'll be on the happy drugs. We get more trouble with drinkers in pubs than with kids taking ecstasy pills at raves.'

We went into a few tents to watch the bands. It was totally black inside, with strobe lights flashing to the beat of the music. There was a makeshift stage and members of a band called TTF were leaping about on it. Ravers with eyes like saucers crowded around them, clutching bottles of water. Their teeth and white T-shirts looked dazzling in the artificial light. We blended in well, as most of them were wearing luminous yellow waistcoats, not too different from our police jackets. One of the ravers approached me, arms flapping, and tried to engage me in a crazy dance. I started laughing and mimicked his movements. Some of the crowd cheered, glad to see that some of the police were human and knew how to have a laugh. Then the raver took my hat off and put it on his head. He'd overstepped the line there and after a couple of minutes I took it back.

It seemed fun to begin with and the atmosphere was very upbeat, but it wasn't quite so much fun being on duty hour after hour. After seven hours we were bussed away to the nearest police office and were allowed either a Chinese meal or fish and chips at the police's expense. It wasn't a special treat because we were doing a fourteen-hour shift; we were due to claim a refreshment allowance and it was cheaper for the police to feed us although normally we paid for our own food.

After our hour's break we were bussed back. It was dark by now and still the music thumped on. The ravers seemed never to run out of energy. Undercover officers moved amongst them trying to identify and arrest dealers. I watched them mingling unobtrusively with the crowd and thought how exciting their job must be, especially compared with ours, which involved a lot of standing around. By the end of fourteen hours I was absolutely whacked, even though I hadn't been dancing. My head was throbbing, and for the next few days all I could hear inside it was that damn music. I've hated it ever since.

On my shift, as on the others, there was a pervasive drinking culture. Keen to fit in, I went along to some of the police nights out. There were relatively few women officers, and the more the men had to drink the more they would come on to us at the end of the night. I would politely decline their over-

tures, which always tended to involve the same chat-up lines
– 'My wife doesn't understand me' really was the most popular! As soon as I heard that one I moved away.

The shift patterns were quite intensive – seven days on and
two days off, with a long weekend off once a month. Because
I didn't get much time off, when I was free I preferred to be
in Glasgow with my family and friends and my boyfriend
Graeme rather than spending too many evenings with these
sleazy cops.

I'd known Graeme since I was sixteen. He was a heating
engineer who had a contract with the council to carry out
maintenance at Summerston. Many of the local tradesmen
were keen to visit our house because three young girls lived
there. Sometimes Graeme would come along to help the joiner
or electrician out even when he was not needed. He was
friends with my mum and dad before he became my boyfriend.
Graeme was very successful as a heating engineer, loved nice
cars and could afford to spend money on them. At that
time he had a Ford RS turbo that he was very proud of. His
office was close to the bus stop I used every day to go to work
in the Intercontinental Hotel and often when he spotted me at
the bus stop he came out of his office and gave me a lift in it.
I couldn't care less what car he drove, but thought that he was
a very nice guy. We spent more and more time together and
then he asked me out.

Most of the people on my shift were from Ayrshire and
they loved going to nightclubs in Greenhill. Because I'd grown
up in Glasgow, where I'd gone out socializing with my older
sisters, and because I'd lived abroad in a big city, the nights
out didn't seem very exciting to me. When I accompanied my

colleagues to pubs or clubs I didn't feel I really fitted in. I returned to my stuffy room in the police station at the end of these evenings feeling empty. I had to walk past officers doing their shifts to get up to my room and it made me feel that I was never off duty.

Greenhill is a very small town, and when I shopped in the local supermarket I sometimes saw people I'd arrested, something that also made me feel that I had no private life away from the police.

By the time I had my eighteen-month appraisal I felt that I understood the basics of the job, had gained vital experience and was handling the work pretty well.

A whole range of senior officers make comments that form part of a trainee's appraisal – sergeant, inspector and superintendent. I sat nervously across the desk from the superintendent as he delivered his verdict on my performance as a police officer.

The superintendent, a squat-faced man with thick brown hair, shuffled a sheaf of papers.

'I hear that you're very competent at your job. You're great at dealing with the public and it says here that you're an asset to the force,' he said.

I beamed. I had had very good feedback from other officers about my performance and was delighted that they had made such positive comments for my appraisal.

'And you look very slim and petite in your uniform.' He looked me up and down, making me feel like a piece of meat.

I was reeling but said nothing. 'What's that got to do with anything?' I thought to myself.

'I've noticed you get dropped off to work in a Porsche

sometimes,' he said, leaning forward. 'Is that your boyfriend who's driving?'

I hadn't realized that I'd been observed.

'Yes,' I said reluctantly. I felt very uneasy that my appearance and my relationship with Graeme seemed to be of at least as much interest to the police as the way I did my work. It made me feel my life was not my own. As far as I was concerned, who I chose to go out with had nothing to do with the police.

'Oh and by the way,' he said, 'now you've done your eighteen months in Greenhill, all new recruits get moved to a sub-divisional office. You're getting moved to Westfield – it's a smaller office with less supervision. I'm sure you'll enjoy it and it'll broaden your experience.'

# Seven

My partner Sergeant Morris slammed the brakes on, the car screeched to a halt and he jumped out brandishing his baton.

'Where's the fire?' I thought to myself. I could just about make out that he was giving a violent beating to someone or something.

'Gotcha!' he cried triumphantly and jumped back into the car.

It was my first time out with him and I was wary of asking what he was doing.

'They bloody foxes keep worrying the sheep,' he said irritably. I was bemused. Clubbing foxes to death wasn't something I'd ever been told should be part of our work, but I'd noticed that his fingernails were black and wondered what he'd been getting up to.

There were just four of us on the shift in the tiny police office in Westfield – a large converted two-storey Victorian house. There were no cells here and any prisoners were taken to Greenhill police station, but we did have two detention rooms and an interview room. Briefings were much more informal. We sat around the table with a cup of tea and read through the crime sheets ourselves instead of having them read out to us as had happened at Greenhill. Memos from senior officers were brought to our attention, along with any changes in the law that we needed to be aware of.

I had been sad to leave Greenhill and missed my partner Gary, but at the same time I jumped at the chance to expand my knowledge of police work. I no longer had a tutor cop and knew that I would have more room to use my own initiative here.

The Westfield office covered the main route between Greenhill and Kilmarnock, a big town in the north of Ayrshire. It also covered three small mining villages. Everybody knew everybody else in these villages, and when we got a call to go to one of them we stood out like a sore thumb. All the houses were built of gloomy grey stone, and when the skies were overcast, which was most of the time, the whole area seemed to be the same miserable shade of slate grey. Ever since the miners' strike in the 1980s there had been deep antipathy towards the police from the villagers.

On my shift, along with Sergeant Morris, was an older officer called Harry who always looked as if he was about to expire. His face had a deathly pallor and his diet was lethal – his wife cooked him a full fried breakfast every morning at 6 am. The first thing he did when he arrived at work was to spend an hour on the toilet. The other officer was called Dean. He was young and keen and had a very possessive wife. He'd been in the job a year longer than me.

When we sat in the kitchen eating our dinner, for some reason Sergeant Morris never brought anything of his own to eat and always stared intently at our food. We all felt obliged to offer him something, but whenever he took one of my chips with his filthy nails I was reluctant to eat any more of them and often gave him the rest. This became a standing joke because it was exactly what he wanted.

A few days after I started, Harry and Dean came towards me holding the office stamp with glints in their eyes. It bore the date and the Strathclyde Police logo. I edged away from them.

'What's going on?' I asked.

'You're getting it. All the girls have to pass an initiation when they come to this office. They get their arse stamped.'

I was totally shocked.

'That'll be bloody right,' I said running away from them. I was wearing a skirt and had started to get really worried.

With his advanced years Harry wasn't quite up to a chase, but Dean ran after me and got me cornered in the police kitchen.

'Don't come near me with that thing or I'll get you done for assault,' I said.

I think that frightened him a bit, but he still came at me and started stamping the back of my white short-sleeved police shirt.

'You bastard,' I shouted, vowing at that moment that I'd get my revenge. A few hours later I found the brightest red lipstick I had in my make-up bag, and when Dean was sitting reading the paper I sneaked up behind him and smeared it all over his sparkling white shirt collar.

'Explain that to your wife,' I beamed.

'Bitch,' he said indignantly. I breathed a sigh of relief. He wouldn't be trying to stamp me again any time soon.

We generally paired up with each other rather than working alone. The law on corroboration in Scotland means that two officers are usually required before somebody can be charged with an offence. One of us was often left to work with the sergeant. Because we were so few in number, sometimes an extra person would be drafted in from another station. I remember being paired with one such officer called Tom who was getting on a bit.

At 1 am Tom and I were called to a housebreaking. The woman who lived there was in bed and heard someone downstairs. She phoned the police from her bedroom and was told to stay on the phone until help arrived. When the call came through on the radio Tom looked terrified and started to drive at speed, but away from the location we'd been given.

'What are you doing? Castle Street is in the opposite direction,' I pointed out.

'It's OK, I know where I'm going,' he said, gripping the steering wheel with sweaty hands. I was anxious about the delay but felt that as I was new to the job it was better not say anything more.

The control room kept calling us asking for our estimated time of arrival. 'What shall I tell them?' I kept saying.

'Don't worry, another car'll get there before us,' he said. I couldn't believe it.

'Romeo Alpha Six where are you?' the controller's voice shouted at us again. I radioed in and gave them the street name.

'You're the nearest car, get there as soon as you can,' said the controller. Tom had no choice but to turn the car round and start driving towards the call. He drove at a snail's pace, but even so when we eventually reached the house we were the first car there. Tom's skin had turned a deathly shade of grey. I thought he was going to have a heart attack. He told me to go round to the back of the house where it was pitch-black and he would wait at the front.

I stood in the garden covering the back door with my baton out, desperately trying to remember what I'd learnt during my basic training and doing my best not to think about what would happen if a knife-wielding burglar came bursting out of the back door. It was the first time I'd been put into a situation where I might have to confront a possibly violent housebreaker and I felt like a terrified wee girl rather than a grown-up police officer in control of the situation. I was petrified because it was so dark and I couldn't trust Tom to protect me.

Then I heard a ruckus at the front of the house, and by the time I ran round there was a guy getting bundled into another police car that must have arrived soon after we did. Tom was sitting in our patrol car taking deep breaths. Because I'd been round the back I had no idea if he had ever left the car at any point. My guess was that he'd probably stayed inside and locked the doors, but I thought it best not to ask.

We spent the rest of the night shift in silence. Thankfully for Tom everything was quiet.

One night Dougie, the officer I'd previously worked with in Greenhill, was sent over from Greenhill to neighbour me because both Harry and Dean were off. I'd met him on my first shift when he had teased Gerry about his rampant sexual appetite.

Well-built and ruddy-faced, Dougie had a reputation for using his baton at every opportunity and senior officers generally seemed quite happy to let him do as he pleased. I didn't see this side of him when we worked together though. He was a lovely man, funny and good-humoured.

We spent most of our shift walking the beat. Dougie was very fond of making coffee and cake stops and we fitted quite a few of those into the shift. But that evening we got a call to go to the aid of two officers who were under attack from the sons of two ex-miners in a village, north of Westfield.

'Send Dougie, he'll sort them out,' Sergeant Morris said.

We set off by car, and as he accelerated hard to get to the village I could see the throb of a vein on his left temple. But by the time we got there the incident had been dealt with. Three young men who looked distinctly worse for wear had been bundled into the back of a police car and were on their way to Greenhill police station.

'Ah well, never mind,' said Dougie, looking disappointed.

I was still living in the grim single quarters at Greenhill police station and driving to Westfield for my shifts, which was a ten-minute journey. Often all of the trainees cooked together to try to make the overheated, institutionalized place feel a bit more homely.

I was particularly friendly with another recruit called Peter. He was about my age but had been in the police a year longer and was very friendly and straightforward.

'How's it going at Westfield, Anne?' he asked me as I stirred a bubbling pan of pasta on the stove.

'I'm quite enjoying it but my sergeant is nuts,' I said,

explaining to him the strange incident with clubbing the fox to death and his horrible black fingernails.

'Ay well, he's a farmer as well as a cop,' said Peter. 'That's why protecting his sheep was more on his mind than protecting the public. I remember him telling me once about how he had bought his daughters a pet lamb and fed it well. They got very attached to it. Then one day they came home and asked where it was and he told them they were having it for dinner!'

I laughed. 'How're you getting on, Peter?'

'Well, I'm neighboured with Gerry, he's my permanent partner now,' he said, rolling his eyes.

'Oh no, what's he been up to?' I asked. 'Has he still got a million girlfriends on the go?'

'Ay, he's got an older one at the moment. She came into the police office in her sussies [suspenders] and he got me rearranging the furniture to find some different positions for them to have sex in. There are only two of us on the shift and he gave me the choice of either watching them at it or joining in.'

'What did you say? Even by Gerry's standards that sounds a bit much.'

'I told Gerry "No thanks" because I had things to do. I had to find ways to keep myself busy for a few hours.'

We both laughed. I decided that I was better off with a partner who was conducting a one-man crusade against foxes than with a lecherous officer who tried to coax me into extra-marital threesomes with him.

At that moment Scott, another recruit living at the police station, walked in. He looked visibly shaken and the atmosphere in the room changed quickly.

'What's wrong, Scott, what's happened?' asked Peter.

'I've just been out with Dougie,' said Scott, his voice trembling. 'We were on foot patrol in the town centre and there was this guy who was going berserk. Dougie hit him a few times with his baton and we called for a car to come so that we could get the guy down to the station. He was still resisting so Dougie hit him a few times in the back of the car and now the guy's made a complaint. Me and the other officers have all got to make a statement about what we saw.'

He sat down and put his head in his hands.

'The cop who was driving said he saw nothing. The female police officer sitting in the front of the car confirmed that she'd seen him hit the prisoner, so now everything hangs on what I say,' he continued with his voice still shaking. 'I know what I saw but I don't want it to be down to me that Dougie loses his job.'

I really felt for Scott. He was in an impossible situation and whatever he did would be wrong.

I was still thinking about his predicament the next day when I was called out to deal with a 'screaming female' at a block of flats in the Westfield area.

When we arrived at the address I could indeed hear a woman screaming. It was a persistent, high-pitched wail.

We had been called by an elderly couple who lived in the flat below. One of them hobbled out to meet us.

'She's up there.' The elderly man pointed to the flat above.

'Thanks,' said Sergeant Morris as we ran past him into the block.

He rapped firmly on the door with his best police knock. The screaming stopped and the door was opened. The occupant was six foot tall with long, dark hair and was wearing a slinky silk dressing gown. It barely covered her huge breasts, but I couldn't take my eyes off her massive feet. Forcing my gaze upwards I saw a prominent Adam's apple.

My jaw was on the floor, but Sergeant Morris kept his cool and said without blinking, 'We've had a complaint about noise coming from this flat and we can hear it from halfway down the street.'

'I cannae help it, it's all the hormone pills I'm taking,' she replied in a voice which was a strange mixture of male and female.

'What's your name?' said Sergeant Morris.

'Cathy,' came the reply.

'No, what's your real name?' he persisted.

'What do you mean? Cathy is my name,' she said, looking offended.

'Are you taking the piss, you're obviously a man,' said Sergeant Morris irritably, his professional veneer slipping.

'My name used to be David but it's Cathy now.'

'Well David, Cathy, whatever your name is, you better keep the noise down or you'll be getting the jail. This is your warning.'

As we walked out of the block of flats I started to giggle. Sergeant Morris looked at me and grinned.

As soon as we climbed back into the patrol car the screaming started again.

'Right, that's it,' said Sergeant Morris, running back towards the flat.

'I can't take much more of that racket,' the elderly woman said, with her dried-up lips quivering. 'It's been going on for days and this is the third time we've had to call you out.'

'No bother, we'll deal with it,' said Sergeant Morris firmly.

We arrested David/Cathy and drove off to the police station. All prisoners are searched by an officer of the same gender, so we couldn't decide whether a male or a female officer should do this search, since she was only halfway through the sex change and still had male genitalia. In the end a compromise was reached – a female officer searched the top half and a male officer continued below the waist!

A couple of days later I found out that Scott had made a statement in support of Dougie. He said that Dougie's actions had been proportionate because the prisoner was resisting arrest. But it seemed that the police had decided Dougie's violent ways were no longer of use to them and they hung him out to dry. He was suspended and later charged with assault and perverting the course of justice. Although I didn't condone Dougie's violence I found out some things about his background. He had problems with his alcoholic wife, who died before his case came to trial, and he hadn't received any support from the police when he was a serving officer, although his domestic difficulties were well known. I also found out that he'd been badly beaten up during a violent fight when he was a new recruit and this was something he'd never quite got over. Scott didn't like the way the police put pressure on him to help them get rid of Dougie. In fact he was so disenchanted with the way the police worked that he got out before he'd completed his probation.

I was beginning to realize that the police were masters of the double standard and that however vulnerable an officer was and however useful they might have been in the past, once a decision had been made to spit an officer out of the system there was not much that officer could do about it.

Shortly after this I reached the end of my two-year probation period. I had received glowing reports from my superiors and was looking forward to the time when my training was complete and I'd be able to take on more responsibility and do my driving course. I'd become much more confident about tackling all different kinds of crime. Incidents like the one with Scott left me feeling concerned about some of the things that went on inside the force, but I loved interacting with the public and felt that I was doing a job where I had a chance to help people.

# Eight

My palms were sweaty and my heart was racing. Tears were running down my cheeks.

'So how are you feeling this week, Anne?' Dr Felicity Arbuthnot asked softly. She was a small slim woman with dark, frizzy, unkempt hair and she kept pushing her thick-framed glasses back up her nose every time they slipped down.

I was sitting in a comfortable leather armchair in a dark room in her house, stuffed from floor to ceiling with shelves of books about psychiatry and psychology and filing cabinets bursting with papers. There was something creepy about this old house full of deep shadows and musty books. I didn't trust anyone, and although Dr Arbuthnot kept on saying that she was here to help me I couldn't bring myself to believe her.

'So how are you feeling this week, Anne?' she asked for the second time. She smiled kindly at me. Her sympathy made my tears flow even faster.

'I'm sorry, I've just been a bit weepy,' I said, shredding the tissue in my hand and then mopping my eyes with it.

'Take your time,' she said. 'Have you been taking your medication?' Her voice was calming and sympathetic.

'Sometimes, when I remember,' I mumbled uncertainly.

'You should try to take it regularly,' she said in a soothing, steady voice. 'It will help you. Is your appetite any better? Are you eating?'

I shook my head and looked down at my stained jeans. I felt too uncomfortable to make eye contact and instead fixed my eyes on a particular coffee splodge on my jeans. I'd been wearing the same pair for a week and simply didn't have the energy to wash them or myself. My hair was greasy and matted. I had no idea how much weight I had lost but all my clothes were hanging off me. My eyes were puffy and everything inside my head felt jumbled up. I struggled to make sense of it all.

'Did you read the leaflets I gave you last week?' she asked.

'No, I can't concentrate on anything,' I said. The tears kept falling. There was nothing I could do to stop them.

'Last week we talked about your work. I feel your distress seems to be closely linked to that. Can you remember when you first had these troubling feelings, as if you were always on edge?'

'Well, I'd had a really successful probation,' I said, taking a deep breath to try to steady my voice. 'About seven or eight months after I'd passed probation I put in for a transfer to Glasgow. My mum wasn't keeping too well and I wanted to buy my own place. I was called for an interview in Glasgow and thought the transfer would be very routine.'

Dr Arbuthnot was looking at me intently through her thick-lensed glasses. The glasses made her eyes look more bulging than they actually were, as if they might pop out of their sockets at any moment.

My tears began again at the memory of the way I was treated. I wiped them away and tried to steady my voice. It sounded weak and papery.

'As soon as I sat across the desk from the superintendent at the police headquarters in Glasgow I sensed that something was wrong,' I said haltingly.

His face was grim as granite and he threw a sheaf of papers at me.

'"How can you even be thinking of asking for a transfer? Look at your brother's convictions." He pointed at the papers he'd thrown at me.'

I paused and took a few sips of the water Dr Arbuthnot offered me, then I continued.

'"What do you mean?" I said to him. I actually felt paralysed with shock.

'"You were sent away for a reason," he replied sharply.

'"I don't understand. I've done nothing wrong," I said. I didn't want him to see me crying but I couldn't help myself. I was totally distraught. "Your brother's just a criminal. There is no way you're getting a transfer," he said.

'"You're making out he's a mass murderer. But his worst crime is petty theft," I said. "And he doesn't even stay at home, he stays with his partner. I don't understand why it should affect me."'

Dr Arbuthnot listened without saying anything. Every now and again she nodded encouragingly. The room was very still and quiet.

'Go on,' she said.

'Then he said, "There are girls your age who are single mums sitting at home with three kids. You're lucky to have a job at all and you shouldn't be complaining about where you're being sent. We could have moved you further away than Greenhill."

'I was particularly shocked because I'd had such a good probation and had no idea that something like this was going to happen.

'"What did you give me a job for if you were going to hold this against me?" I asked him. He couldn't answer me.'

'How did that make you feel?'

'Terrible. I was made to feel like a criminal and he also made me feel that my family were bad people. It was as if I was being asked to choose between my family and the police. For me my family came first no matter what. He told me I couldn't visit my family home and that I wouldn't make a satisfactory police officer. I couldn't believe what I was hearing. I felt that the whole thing was so unjust and that I was being victimized. He ended the interview by saying, "Go back to your station at Greenhill."

'There was no way that I was going to do that. I didn't have another shift for a few days and I went straight home to my mum.'

'And what did she think?' asked Dr Arbuthnot.

'She was totally appalled, and seeing how upset I was made her feel very upset too.

'"Who do those police think they are?" my mum said indignantly. She felt they were belittling her family. My dad was furious too. He continued to worry about me being in the police. "Why are you still doing that job? You should just get out. You could do anything you wanted," he said to me.'

'What happened next?' The room was darkening as the

afternoon turned to evening but she did not move to turn on the lights.

'I decided to look for another job. I didn't want to be treated like that. I realized that however good I was at my job it didn't matter because the police would still hold my brother's past against me for the rest of my career.'

'Did you start to look at the police in a different way after that?' she asked.

'Yes, I felt I'd been naive because I hadn't seen that they were holding this against me. I'd thought they were fairer than that. But I'd been very gullible to think that what my brother had done wouldn't affect me. I thought if I worked hard I would be rewarded for being a good police officer, not held back for having a brother with previous convictions. After that I was much more wary of them. There's a phrase the police use a lot: "That's just the way we do things here." It's the response they give whenever anyone challenges them, and the superintendent threw it at me. I found it very sinister.'

I began sobbing again. Talking about it had made me relive it. 'I was all set to leave the police,' I continued. 'But then out of the blue, about six months later, I got called in by the chief inspector at Westfield to say that I'd got the transfer to Glasgow on condition that I didn't live at home. I never found out why they changed their minds.'

# Nine

I pushed open the swing doors of the briefing room at Williamstone police station in Glasgow's west end. I felt so much more
confident than when I had walked into the briefing room on
my first-ever shift, but I was still nervous because once again
I was the new girl.

This time there were fixed benches all facing in one direction, so I couldn't make the same faux pas as on my first shift,
sitting in someone else's seat. The room started to fill up.
Although I hadn't seen these particular officers before they
looked very similar to the ones I'd worked with at other stations – overweight and, at the beginning of their shift, still only
half dressed. They broke off from their raucous jeering banter
for a few seconds to look me up and down and then resumed
whatever it was that they were discussing so intently. At first
I couldn't work out what they were talking about then it suddenly dawned on me.

'Yeh, I have to shave my balls,' said one.

'No you don't, you prick,' said another.

'You better watch because sometimes the tubes reconnect
and she can end up up the duff.'

'Think twice aboot it mate. Sheila insisted I got one after we had the kids but now I'm wi' Linda she wants weans and I'm trying to reverse it.'

It seemed that almost every male officer in the room had had a vasectomy, and they were doing their best to scare an officer who was obviously about to have the operation. I couldn't believe that all the officers were sitting there discussing something like this – it reminded me of women sitting around discussing their periods.

The conversation came to a sudden halt when the shift inspector walked in accompanied by two sergeants. As the inspector began to talk I noticed that he had a facial twitch and that he ended almost every sentence with the words 'okey dokey'.

I tried my best to forget about the cruel words of the superintendent at police headquarters about my brother and made an effort to fit into the shift. I felt as if I was starting again because I didn't know anyone, although I could recognize certain classic features amongst the officers in the room, notably the cynical expressions and the bigoted language. The shift gossip that day was about an officer called Lesley Brown who had gone off sick. Every officer I spoke to couldn't wait to tell me that her sick leave had begun after she made a complaint against her shift inspector. He'd been sexually harassing her for months. Nothing had happened to him, but she'd been moved onto this shift and had been off sick the whole time.

'She might win the battle but she'll never win the war,' said one of the officers, raising his eyebrows.

I felt angry and wanted to say something but decided that because it was my first day it was best to keep my mouth shut.

Soon after my arrival I was sent on a week-long police driving course and learnt how to drive safely at speed, providing a commentary on my movements for the radio as I drove – which isn't easy. Reversing round cones and driving into a skidpan were two new skills that I'd picked up by the end of the week.

I felt much happier working in the west end, an area I was familiar with and which was very lively. Part of it consists of the affluent leafy suburbs of Hyndland and Dowanhill, with Victorian red stone buildings inhabited by upwardly mobile professionals. Byers Road and Ashton Lane have quirky boutiques and trendy bars. The west end also houses Glasgow University, which has about 30,000 students whose bedsits fill the surrounding Hillhead area. Partick is a more working-class area, as are Yoker and Scotstoun, further west, which have many blocks of high-rise flats and high levels of unemployment. It was here that a lot of the drugs raids took place.

Bit by bit I found myself getting better at observing crime and picking up on local trends. I was also getting good feedback from colleagues and felt that I was becoming a good police officer. If I was in a shop I could pick out the potential shoplifter, who tended to be watching the security guard intently. I became adept at spotting when a drug-dealer was surreptitiously passing a wrap of heroin to a user, or when a bag-dipper was watching someone's bag in preparation for swiping something from it, or maybe even lifting the bag itself. I sometimes observed people walking very slowly down the street stopping at every parked car and peering through the windows to see if there was anything worth stealing. I developed a sixth sense about when people were doing something or were about to do something that they shouldn't have been doing. It was a skill that came with experience.

Although there was more crime in Glasgow than in Green-hill, many of the crimes were similar. I'd been with the police for three and a half years now and was twenty-four, and I felt I was now a real police officer, able to handle most situations I found myself in.

At the beginning I'd kept my head down and tried to learn the job, but now I was beginning to carve out my own iden-tity as an officer. I was more confident about expressing my opinions, and if I thought something was wrong I was pre-pared to speak out about it.

I was on a night shift a few weeks after I moved to Glasgow and was neighboured up with two officers called Phil and Brian in a seven-seater police van. They were an odd pair. Brian was much older and more experienced than Phil, who had just completed his probation. They seemed to get along well. They gabbled away about the Rangers match the day before and obviously shared the same views about their team. I was content to sit quietly in the back, my eyes peeled for any-thing suspicious. Phil was telling Brian that he was feeling nervous because his wife was pregnant for the first time and was due to give birth any day.

'Don't worry about it son,' said Brian. 'Just don't make the same mistake I did.'

'What do you mean?' asked Phil.

'Well, I turned up at the hospital to witness ma eldest being born. The doc handed me a gown to change into so I did. Except he forgot to tell me not to take my clothes off, so there

I was, big bare arse hanging oot the back. Janice was mortified.'

We all laughed. 'I can't believe you did that,' I said, joining in with the conversation.

'Whit the hell's that?' said Brian suddenly, cutting the childbirth conversation short. We looked out of the front window and could see a man walking down the street. He was about six foot tall, a body-builder type, and was wearing a hooded grey sweatshirt. My eyes were drawn to his bottom half. He was wearing a short grey school skirt, high heels and stockings.

Brian stopped the van alongside the man.

'Oy you! Come here a minute,' said Brian, taking control. Phil glued himself to Brian's side. They looked like a pair of vultures waiting to pounce.

I looked more closely at the man. His head was shaved and from the waist up he looked very masculine. The contrast between his top and bottom half gave him quite a bizarre look.

'What's your name?' asked Brian.

'Jason Gates,' said the man in a deep voice that matched his top half.

Brian quizzed him about where he was from and about why he was dressed the way he was. Gates said he lived outside Glasgow and that he was on his way home from a stag night where his friends had dressed him up. Even I found this hard to believe, and Phil and Brian were looking unconvinced. Eventually we let him go, but as we got back into the police van it was obvious that Phil and Brian felt they couldn't just leave it at that.

'Ah'm no happy aboot letting him go,' said Brian.

'He's not done anything wrong,' I insisted.

'I'm with you, Brian,' piped up Phil.

'I wonder if he's wearing anything underneath that skirt,' said Brian.

I seriously wondered what was going on in his head. That hadn't even crossed my mind.

'That's it,' Brian declared. 'If he's got nothing under that skirt he's definitely getting the jail.'

He pulled up alongside Jason Gates again. Phil and Brian approached him whilst I hung back. I watched as Jason lifted his skirt to reveal a pair of ladies' red satin knickers. The knickers saved the day and they let him go.

After the break Brian and I went out on patrol. Phil went off duty early because he had court in the morning. This time I drove.

'So how long have you been in the job?' I asked.

'Eighteen years,' he replied. 'I was in CID for five.'

'Oh right. What happened?'

'I got shafted. Some supervisor decided he didn't like me so he wrote me a bad appraisal and said I needed to go back on the streets. He played golf with my boss Superintendent McDonald. Next thing I know I'm back on the shift. So what did you do wrong?'

I was taken aback. I wasn't aware that I'd done anything wrong.

'What do you mean?' I asked.

'Well, the guys have been making phone calls to your old division to find out why you got moved.'

'I asked for the move,' I said indignantly, irritated that assumptions had been made about me.

'Ay right,' said Brian, obviously not believing me.

It was 4 am and we were driving through Kelvingrove Park, a huge open space that was frequented at night by gay men and young guys who robbed them. As we drove along I could make out a female figure ahead of us. I pulled the car up alongside her and wound down the window.

'What are you doing walking alone through the park at this hour?' I said. 'It isn't safe.'

She was American and answered vaguely, 'Oh I was just on my way home from a party.'

'Jump in, we'll take you home,' I said. This wasn't part of the job description, but when I saw young women making themselves vulnerable like that I thought it could just as easily have been me or one of my friends, and I didn't like to think of what might happen to them.

After we dropped her safely home Brian turned to me annoyed. 'Are we a fucking taxi service?'

'No, of course not. It's for her safety. She's not even from here. Would you want your daughter walking through there in the middle of the night?'

'Fucking waste of time, we should be catching criminals,' Brian said.

'Yeah, like some guy wearing a school skirt. What crime is that?' I said. I was furious with him and felt I was experienced enough to speak up and say how I felt. He just grunted and looked the other way.

I began to pick young women up regularly whenever I saw one walking alone in the middle of the night who I felt was vulnerable. I'd drawn up my own set of rules about the circumstances under which I'd stop and pick up a lone woman.

If she was on an open road where there were no buses or taxis, or if she was in a rough area and stuck out like a sore thumb because she obviously wasn't from there and as a result seemed scared, I picked her up. It was my own personal crime prevention strategy.

I'd been stranded once myself as a teenager. I'd lost my bus fare home after an evening at a club, and when I started walking home I was leered at by a passing taxi-driver in a black cab. He was driving past me on the other side of the road, rolled his window down and started shouting, 'Get them off.'

He slowed down as if to do a U-turn and I ran as fast as I could in the other direction. I was scared to flag down a taxi after that, but eventually I found a black cab driven by a woman. I got in and told her what had happened. She asked me if I'd got his registration but I hadn't. It was because of what was possibly a near-miss for me that I felt sympathetic when I saw young women who appeared to be in a similar predicament.

Some of the young women seemed quite surprised when I stopped. They couldn't believe the police would do something like that. I was pleased to be able to show them that the police could help protect members of the public who were vulnerable as well as catching criminals.

A few weeks later I was sitting in the report-writing room catching up with my paperwork when the door opened and a plainclothes officer swaggered in. I didn't know his name but I'd seen him with a group of other officers speeding out of the back yard in an unmarked car like characters out of a TV cop show.

'Are you available to help us out with a turn? We need a

female,' he said, speaking fast. A turn was a major search of a house or a person.

'I'd like to, but I'm tied up with paperwork and the sergeants want me to do female turnkey second half.'

'I'll speak to your sergeant,' he said arrogantly.

'Who is it you're going to turn anyway?' I asked.

'It's the McPhersons at Kingsway.'

I stared at him blankly. The name meant nothing to me. He gave me a withering look that made me feel as if I was stupid.

'What an arsehole,' I thought to myself. I didn't hear anything more about helping out with the turn and carried on with my paperwork.

I'd split up from my boyfriend before I moved to Glasgow and wasn't allowed to live with my parents, so instead I rented a room in a friend's place. I think he started to wonder what he'd let himself in for when an inspector was sent round to check that his flat was 'decent'. It's normal for the police to run a check on the address of their recruits, but a home visit was more unusual. He was pretty nervous about the process, but luckily there weren't any problems. We got on well together but I really wanted to buy my own place and started looking almost straight away. After about six months I found a lovely two-bedroomed Victorian flat, with cornices, original wooden floors and fireplaces and a huge freestanding bath. It was near my mum and dad's, and instantly felt like home.

I was really excited about spending my first Christmas in the flat, but in the end it was memorable for other reasons. Christmas morning was freezing cold, with snow falling, and I was on patrol alone. There were only a few staff on duty and the mood in the office was upbeat and jovial. It was usually quiet, as most premises were closed and the criminals generally took a day off. I liked doing the early shift on Christmas Day. We got paid double and I finished at 3 pm, which meant that I could get home early enough to enjoy the rest of the day with my family. For us Christmas was a big occasion.

I had started my shift at 7 am and now it was just after 8. The radio crackled and I received a call to deliver a death message. It had come from a different force and wasn't very detailed. It just gave the victim's name, vague circumstances about what had happened and a helpline number for Northern Constabulary. My heart sank. It was bad enough being the bearer of such grim news on an ordinary day, but today it seemed particularly cruel to have to tell someone a loved one had died. It made me think of my own family as I drove towards the call. I had been looking forward to getting off duty and going round to my mum's house for our traditional family get-together with lots of food. As I knocked on the door, though, my appetite vanished. A young woman appeared. She was probably just a few years younger than me, and as soon as she saw me standing at the door in my uniform a shadow crossed her face.

'Are you Alison Burns?' I asked, my heart pounding.

'Yes, has something happened?'

'Do you mind if I come in?' I said. She gestured for me to follow her into her living room. My hands were trembling with nerves as I sat down.

'I'm afraid to tell you that your dad has been in an accident and has been killed. I'm very sorry.'

She looked at me disbelievingly for a few moments, then

became hysterical and started screaming. I tried unsuccessfully to calm her down.

'What happened?' she sobbed.

I looked at the bit of paper I had with me.

'I'm sorry, I don't have a lot of information for you because it happened in another force. All I know is that he fell off a roof. I've got a number here that you can call to get more details.'

I hugged her. She seemed inconsolable.

'Can I call anyone for you, can I make you a cup of tea?'

I had to do something because if I sat there any longer I knew I was going to cry, and that wouldn't help her. I wished I could take away some of the pain she was feeling. It was especially distressing for her because I had to go through the lengthy process of finding out more details about her family and their whereabouts. I was reluctant to leave her because she was in such a state, so I stayed with her for a few hours, until I got another call on my radio to go and check an alarm going off at a shop. I often felt that we couldn't spend enough time with victims of crime and bereaved people.

I headed back to my flat at the end of my shift to get changed out of my uniform. Because the place had very high ceilings I'd bought a big Christmas tree. The scent of pine needles greeted me as soon as I opened my front door. My fireplace was filled with Christmas cards and there was a pile of nicely wrapped presents for my family waiting under the tree. I had a shower, picked up the presents and drove to my parents' home.

As I walked in the familiar sound of Bing Crosby wafted

over to me. My dad always played his music on Christmas Day.

The men were having a beer and the women were in the kitchen prodding the turkey and turning over the roast potatoes. My mum walked into the living room and gave me a big hug. 'Happy Christmas,' she said.

'Happy Christmas to you too,' I replied and gave her a kiss. I greeted the rest of the family, hugging and kissing everyone. My dad put a glass of bubbly in my hand.

'How was your day, hen?' he asked, smiling broadly.

'OK,' I said, keen to change the subject about how I'd spent Christmas morning. My mum had gone back into the kitchen to check on the turkey and all the trimmings. 'I'll go and see if Mum needs a hand,' I said.

My sister Kim had laid everything out for the Christmas lunch and was plopping Brussels sprouts onto the eleven plates.

'Have you got everything under control or do you want me to do anything?' I asked.

'Just make sure everybody's got a drink,' she said.

Big flashing stars and snowmen had been pasted to the front window of the living room and there were lots of decorations festooned across the ceiling. I felt my heart warm a little as I watched three of my young nieces and nephews running around pulling crackers. But then my mind went back to the poor girl I'd just delivered the death message to. There would be no Christmas cheer for her this year.

Everybody had their party hats on. A cracker was shoved in my face so that I could put one on too. They'd waited until I arrived to exchange presents, and we all began peeling off the festive wrapping paper and exclaiming that the presents we'd received were just what we'd been wanting for ages.

Then we all sat round a big table. My dad got up to put Frank Sinatra's Christmas hits on. Lynne took lots of photos. My two three-year-old nephews looked cute in their Santa outfits. Glasses of champagne were passed around and everyone laughed at the stupid jokes in the crackers.

After a few mouthfuls of turkey I found I couldn't manage any more. My family's chatter buzzed happily around me but I didn't feel able to join in. I realized that I was starting to take my work home with me and that a gulf was developing between me and my family and friends who were not involved in the job. Usually I would have been the life and soul of the party, but my work was changing me. I was turning in on myself. I could see my mum watching me with a concerned look on her face.

As the party games kicked off I looked around at my family's happy faces but couldn't shake off the sadness I felt for the young woman I'd had to give the bad news to. Keen not to dampen the atmosphere, I decided to leave early, which was unlike me, and headed home to my flat. I was looking forward to starting a new job in community policing after Christmas. At least there I wouldn't have to deliver any more death messages.

# Ten

'Get back,' he screamed.

The next thing I knew I was lying face-down gasping for air. The weight of a sixteen-stone man bore down on me, his knee dug into my back and his hand held me down. I felt dizzy and my heart was pounding. I was no match for him. He held his hand out and pulled me back on to my feet.

'Are you all right?'

I caught my breath. 'Yes,' I wheezed.

Then it was my turn to do the same to him.

We were in the gym on the first floor of the police station. It reminded me of my gym at school with its scuffed wooden floor, tall ceiling and windows set high up in the walls. There were male and female changing rooms and a couple of pool tables in the corner. At lunchtimes some of the senior officers played badminton there.

Once a year we had a one-day refresher course in baton training. When I joined, the old baton given to female officers was being phased out. It was a small wooden pen-like object, the kind of thing you'd see Punch hitting Judy with at a puppet show. I was relieved not to get one because I couldn't imagine what use it would be in a conflict. Instead I was given the same-size truncheon as the men, still sturdy enough to beat people or to smash windows. Later these were replaced with new, side-handled, aluminium PR 24s – modern, extendable batons, which made a piercing noise when we flicked them out to their full twenty-four inches. We'd been encouraged to hide our old wooden truncheons in a deep, secret pocket in our trousers so as not to appear confrontational to the public. Many of us were proud of the scratches on the truncheons, regarding them as our battle scars. In contrast the new batons were much more aggressive. We kept them in a visible pouch on a special belt we were issued with. All of a sudden we were no longer bobbies on the beat but had been transformed into (literally) hard-hitting American cops. Although the baton felt more threatening it was reassuring to have something that offered me more protection than our old wooden weapons.

There were lots of jokes about size when they were first handed out because some of the smaller officers were given twenty-two-inch batons. And it didn't help that the side handle resembled a phallic symbol.

On the course this day, ten of us from different departments were paired off. Two constable instructors led the session. Both were physically fit and had been on a training course to teach us baton skills. There was a lot of banter, particularly amongst the older, more seasoned officers, about the training. Nobody took it seriously and it was regarded as a day off work. All we had to do was show that we could perform certain moves with our batons and handcuffs, then sign a piece of paper to cover the chief constable's back that we'd received training.

We were shown a series of different stances, defensive and attacking moves. A diagram of a body highlighted the parts that were acceptable to strike, such as the arms and legs. There were red areas that we were supposed not to strike unless we were in serious danger, such as the head, genitals and internal organs.

We were reminded of the dangers of asphyxiating prisoners by piling on top of them when they were face-down, although the rules were not always followed and some deaths in police custody were found by inquests to be due to asphyxiation while prisoners had been held face-down. We learnt plenty of baton-specific jargon, phrases to use for court reports like, 'I extended my baton . . .' and that we had 'used reasonable and necessary force'. In reality these rules and regulations went out of the window when we were faced with real-life situations. If someone pulled a knife out it was human nature for police officers to react on impulse rather than consulting the manual first. When I was first issued with the new baton I tried one of the moves, called an inside spin. I approached a man who was wanted for an earlier theft. My baton was extended and I held it behind my leg. As I got to arm's length of him I quickly pushed the long side of the baton underneath his arm and at the same time pushed his wrist up behind his back using the side handle. Then I got the handcuffs on him. He was shocked because he didn't see it coming. I was shocked because I'd performed the move successfully.

We were given CS gas canisters and went outside to spray them on each other's faces so that we knew what the effects would be. I stood out in the back yard of the police office squeezing my eyes tightly shut.

'Open your eyes, it's meant to be natural,' said the officer who was about to spray me. I opened my eyes a chink and was blinded at once by the stinging spray. My eyes started to water and I felt light-headed but the sensation subsided after a few minutes. We were told that it had no effect at all on some people, usually people who were under the influence of alcohol, which was hardly good news.

About a year after moving to Glasgow I'd applied to join the community police. I felt I'd enough experience working on the uniform shifts and wanted to move my career on by trying a different department. There were about ten constables and a sergeant in our department, and because it was such a small team I was the only woman, but everyone was friendly. I loved my new job – I was no longer working night shifts and had more time to spend, as the job title indicates, interacting with the community. It was a relief not to have to deal with the kind of human misery I had to tackle during my first few years in the police. While my job still involved arresting criminals, I felt I had more of a chance to make a positive difference to people's lives, sorting out pests who had made their lives a misery.

I was glad of the chance to get to know a smaller area really well, to earn the trust of the local residents and make myself accepted as part of the community. I gained a better understanding of the socio-economic issues that affected people's daily lives rather than just looking at everything from a purely criminal perspective.

I gave a lot of talks in schools and hospitals about crime prevention and felt that if I could persuade just one person to be more careful about where they put their bag down or one pupil not to get involved with drugs my work was worthwhile.

This was one of my happiest periods in the police. I often worked alone, attended lots of meetings with different members of the local community and was free to use my own initiative.

The downside of this job was that we were enlisted for all sorts of public order duties because we mainly did day shifts. One of my least favourite tasks was policing the annual Orange march in July, a Protestant occasion. I stood alongside the marchers listening to their chants.

'Hello, hello, we are the Billy boys, hello, hello, you'll know us by our noise,' the Orange flute band blasted out.

Like all Glaswegians, I had been aware of sectarianism from an early age. As a child of five I went to the local Catholic school because it was all there was. But when a Protestant school was built nearby, Lynne and I were told we had to go there instead. I found out later that the priest wasn't happy about us staying in the Catholic school because we weren't practising Catholics. I couldn't understand why something like that mattered. To my mind the only difference between the two schools was that at the Catholic school we said a prayer in the morning while at the Protestant school we didn't.

Things got even worse when I started secondary school. I had to make a twenty-five-minute bus journey to the Protestant school, and yet when a Catholic secondary school, St John Paul, was built around the corner from where we lived they refused to accept Lynne and me because we weren't Catholics. Every time we took the bus home the kids who sat upstairs sang rowdy Orange songs. I wasn't interested in that kind of thing so I sat downstairs. When we reached Summerston the pupils from the Catholic school threw stones at the bus, and often mini riots ensued.

I joined a Protestant girls' brigade along with a lot of girls when I was nine. I went along to church every Saturday morning and learnt how to march. Much as I enjoyed feeling part of something, I found the church itself creepy and only went for about a year. The church was across the road from the Orange Lodge and we often heard the bands practising.

I'd attended small marches in Greenhill, but this was the first time I was policing such a big and potentially violent event. Now I stood with a group of police officers waiting for the trouble that was almost certain to break out at some point during the march.

We were all wearing our luminous yellow jackets. At these events the philosophy was to flood the place with police and make ourselves as conspicuous as possible. None of us had a particular role to play. We were just anonymous bodies filling up the ranks. So long as the sea of yellow jackets were visible I was sure that our superiors wouldn't have minded if the bodies inhabiting them had been volunteer grannies rather than able-bodied police officers. It was just a numbers game.

In fact the majority of police in Glasgow were Protestant, and one officer told me that when he joined about a decade earlier, all the Catholic recruits were put together in one police office. I'd seen myself many years later how just appearing to be the wrong religion could cause problems. It was obvious when we policed these marches that some officers were more enthusiastic than others about the task because they had sympathies with the politics of the Orange Lodge and were members of the Protestant Masons. It seemed odd to me that a few of the officers who were low-ranking constables held high positions such as Grand Master in the Masonic lodge, while some senior officers were lower in the Masonic pecking order. Often these constables had cushy desk jobs and were allowed to do as they liked at work. They appeared to be the right-hand men of senior officers, enjoying some kind of professional privilege.

I looked around at the band, which was led by a drummer with an outsize belly. Behind him, dressed in tunics and sashes, were three older men in black suits who were obviously leaders in the order. They were carrying long poles bearing the lodge insignia. Then came a series of other bands, mainly flute bands, grouped according to the colour of their tunics. Dispersed between these were rows of women wearing white suits and coloured sashes. Some of them looked quite old and frail, and I wondered how they were going to make it from Partick to Glasgow Green, a march that took two or three hours.

A crowd of male supporters followed after, most of them bare-chested and clutching cans of cheap super lager, cider and bottles of Buckfast. Our duty was to march beside them in single file and protect them from the traffic, because they marched on the road. We usually had to deal with trouble along the way – the windows of Catholic pubs were targeted and anyone who dared to cross the path of the marchers risked getting their head kicked in. Often groups of Catholics would start up trouble by throwing bottles and stones into the midst of thousands of marchers.

This tradition of marching had started in Northern Ireland many years before and had now become fully integrated into Scottish society. The noise of the band drowned out most conversation, but occasionally I heard snatches of verbal abuse. 'Kick the fuck out of him, he's just broke the line,' said one Orange marcher when a member of the public tried to cross the road in between them rather than wait an hour for them to pass. When we heard comments like that we moved to protect the person crossing the road.

We had to march back with them too, and because they'd spent the day drinking in Glasgow Green and the weather was hot we were weary, sunburnt and frustrated by the time we set off again. Fights kept breaking out all around and police were constantly being taken out of the line to arrest people, usually for drink-fuelled violence.

Most of the marchers had no idea why they were marching. The original purpose seemed to have been forgotten and now it was an excuse for an extended booze-up and to make their mark on the street. I had no bias against Protestants – I would have felt exactly the same if it had been Catholics marching. But I felt that events like this one intensified sectarian conflict.

It would have made more sense if people had marched through a park, so that the whole of the city centre wasn't disrupted. But it would have been a political nightmare to get the marchers to change their traditional route, and there seemed to be no great appetite for change amongst many of the senior police officers who were Orange sympathizers.

Sectarianism reared its head in football too. Rangers were Glasgow's 'Protestant' team and Celtic the 'Catholic' one. My dad was an avid fan of Celtic. I was a tomboy when I was little and I loved to go to the games with him. Because I was small he would lift me over the turnstiles without paying for me. But he stayed away from Celtic–Rangers matches because he was worried about trouble.

Paul Gascoigne inflamed an already sensitive situation when he was signed to Rangers: he mimed playing a flute as though he was in an Orange Order marching band, without understanding the implications. He hadn't realized how much trouble it would cause, but there was an outcry from Celtic fans and from the media. These players were supposed to be setting an example, not making things worse. When Mark Walters played for Rangers in his debut game against Celtic, some of the Celtic fans threw bananas on the pitch and sang racist songs because he was the only black player in the Rangers team. It stirred up a scandal.

Both of these players were English and didn't understand what a powerful force sectarianism was in Scotland. Although the incident involving Mark Walters was racist there was a sectarian element to it too.

I saw this all the time when I worked at football matches. Usually around thirty minibuses, each carrying around twelve officers, arrived at the ground before the match started. Each busload of officers was dropped off at designated points around the ground. Around thirty mounted police were stationed outside the ground, and vanloads of riot-trained support police were parked up in side streets. They would stay in the vans until they were called to deal with particular disturbances that broke out during or after the match. A police office was set up underneath the ground to process fans who were arrested, and there were frequently hundreds of arrests at a game.

Often I was posted at an exit point in the stadium with

another officer. Before the game even started there were many arrests in the streets because of clashes between rival fans. Officers moved into a range of positions in and around the ground in preparation for the start of the match. Some police officers lined the pitch.

Inside the ground the atmosphere was terrifying. There was tension in the air and an undercurrent of menace. I would pray for a draw so that there wouldn't be trouble after the game. At many of the grounds there were eight stands in a circle around the pitch. There were stairs about the width of a goal post in between each stand, and the fans in any stand were divided from those in the next one by metal fencing.

The worst posting to get was on the stairs between two rival sets of fans. They shouted abuse at each other and threw coins. The law had been changed to ban supporters from bringing bottles or cans of drink into the ground, so thankfully we didn't have them lobbed over our heads. The noise at the match was deafening and we had to duck as the coins, hurled by one set of fans towards their rivals, flew above us. We had to ignore most of the abuse that was directed at us because we were very much in the minority at these matches – some three hundred of us to 50,000 fans. In reality there was very little we could do except to try our best to control situations as they arose. Sometimes officers got hit in the face outside the ground with bottles, bricks or coins and suffered injuries severe enough to require them to be taken away for medical treatment.

Some officers got a lot of job satisfaction from arresting fans of the team they didn't support, and would brag about their arrest numbers.

As matches drew to an end tension grew amongst the police officers. After the game we had to escort fans away from the ground and keep a close eye on them to prevent fighting.

One time I was given a job to do at Parkhead in the east end of Glasgow, Celtic's home ground. A decision was made by the officer in charge to divert the Celtic fans leaving the ground on to a route that passed the oldest Rangers pub in the east end, called the Loudon Bar. It was heavily decorated on the outside in red, white and blue. The pub was heaving because Rangers had won and most of the drinkers had spilled out onto the street. We were stationed between the two sets of fans, so when both sides started lobbing missiles over our heads towards each other, some of them were bound to hit us before they reached their targets. I felt vulnerable and absolutely terrified. No amount of baton training would help, and I'd had no public order training with shields and helmets. I just wasn't equipped to deal with the situation. We were completely at the mercy of the crowd. Images kept flashing through my mind of some frenzied fan smashing a beer bottle into my face and leaving me in agony, bloodied and scarred for life.

There was an inspector from the mounted branch behind us who made a decision for us to force the Rangers supporters further down the street to try to separate them from the Celtic fans. I was lined up shoulder to shoulder with other officers.

I ended up getting pushed towards some of the Rangers fans because I was facing the Rangers pub. Now I was sandwiched between the two sets of fans with no room for manoeuvre. The inspector's decision had proved to be a dangerous one because we ended up pushing the Rangers supporters into a Catholic area. They rebelled and turned on us. Panic rose inside me and sheer terror clutched at my throat, but I knew it was vital not to let the angry fans smell my fear. I was responding to this critical situation as a human being bent on survival rather than as a police officer, and I couldn't help feeling outraged that the inspector had put me and other officers in such jeopardy.

I knew that I and my fellow officers were completely trapped. Bottles continued to fly and I could hear officers shouting, 'This is fucking terrible.' It was safe enough for the inspector mounted on his big horse and carrying his shield. He wasn't even in the crowd: he was further down the street. Given the chance to speak to him I would have told him exactly what I thought of his plan and tried to talk him out of it, because it was putting both fans and officers in danger. As he was out of reach and out of contact we were left to our own devices.

I thought I was either going to get crushed to death or thumped to death.

'If you fucking push me one more time I'll put your fucking face in,' one of the Rangers fans said to me. He was a dark-haired man, about six foot two, and plastered with tattoos. I could tell by his face that it was no idle threat.

I looked him in the eye: 'I'm really sorry, I'm not trying to push you, I'm getting pushed from behind. I'm just trying to do my job.' I knew that persuasion was my only chance. He seemed convinced by my calm and confident act, even though I felt anything but that. He backed off and I breathed a huge sigh of relief.

This stand-off went on for some time until most of the

Celtic supporters had passed. Eventually we managed to clear the area. I was shaking with terror and many of the fans must have felt the same. I knew how close we'd come to having serious casualties, and it was all over a game of football.

There was one particularly horrifying incident that stuck in my mind whenever I was on duty at a match between these two teams. It was sectarianism taken to its most violent and bigoted extreme. Sixteen-year-old Mark Scott, a Celtic fan, had just finished watching his team beat Partick Thistle and was on his way home with two friends. A group of Rangers fans including Jason Campbell, whose father and uncle were Protestant terrorist paramilitaries, began to scream abuse at them. Mark and his friends didn't react but Campbell sneaked up behind them, grabbed Mark and slashed his throat, fatally wounding him. Campbell then raced home, showered, changed, and later that evening went to stay with friends in Greenock. But in the first hours after the incident police received more than fifty phone calls naming him as the killer. The next day he gave himself up and he was jailed for life in March 1996.

I couldn't make sense of the knowledge that an innocent schoolboy walking home after a match and making no trouble had been murdered simply because he supported the 'wrong' team. I had never been able to understand the fierce tribal loyalties that ran not only through football but through so many other areas of Glasgow life. The enmity began at school, where some Catholic and Protestant kids refused to play with each other. And the seeds of antagonism sown in childhood had grown into poisonous plants by the time these children reached adulthood. It seemed that some people needed hatred of the outsider to inflate their own sense of themselves. In other communities across the world hatreds between one group and another had different labels and different causes, but they amounted to the same thing: 'You're different from me and my gang, so I don't like you and I'm entitled to hurt you.'

# *Eleven*

When I wasn't on duty at football matches I loved community policing and spent a lot of time patrolling the west end with its quirky shops and friendly people. It was great being back in Glasgow, my home city. My partner on the beat was called Stevie. He was a good police officer and we got on like a house on fire. We often sat in the canteen of the Safeways supermarket sipping tea during our breaks. Now and then a fight would break out when a security guard grabbed a shoplifter and he tried to get away, and our tea breaks were often interrupted when staff called us over to help. They were happy to have us around – it made them feel safer.

One Christmas Eve we were called to break up a fight between two middle-aged women laden with shopping bags who had gone to war over the last turkey. They were much more aggressive and determined than the shoplifters.

After I'd been in the community police for a few months I started to recognize particular crime patterns. The same people cropped up again and again committing the same kinds of crimes. If one of the local drug addicts was withdrawing, desperate for cash for a fix, all I had to do was follow him fifty yards down the road and wait for him to commit a crime. Once, as we were walking along Byers Road, we saw a well-known local addict coming out of a Thorntons shop, his jacket pockets stuffed with stolen chocolates. He saw us coming, ran back into the shop and started unloading his loot back on to the shelves. Stevie and I were in hysterics – it was the first time I'd ever seen a shoplifter put anything back! He still got arrested though, because there was a warrant out for him.

We spent a lot of time sauntering up and down our patch just keeping an eye on things. Stevie was older than me, but had a real baby face which he got teased about and must have got him teased at school as well. He had a crush on a large-breasted woman called Margaret who worked in the local optician's. It didn't stop him from noticing other women though, his eyes firmly fixed on their bums, particularly in the summer months when they wore fewer clothes. I was forever shaking my head at him and jokingly accusing him of being a pervert. He always took that with good humour.

But Stevie had a bee in his bonnet about improperly parked vehicles, and his passion for towing away offenders was the one thing we fought over. I was almost never in favour of towing away unless a vehicle was causing a serious obstruction, and always tried to trace the owner before taking such a drastic step. I'd had my own car towed away once when I'd parked it on a yellow line in the city centre for two minutes while I popped into a shop to get my sister a birthday present. I'd got a fright when I came out of the shop and thought my car had been stolen, and I didn't want to put someone else through all that trouble and expense unless it was absolutely necessary.

One time Stevie even towed away an army tank, despite my protestations that he should leave it where it was. I never found out what it was doing parked in Kelvin Way near the university.

'Don't be a bloody idiot, that's an army tank,' I said, when I realized that Stevie was making a call to get it towed. 'I don't think it'll go down too well.'

It didn't. The police were sent a huge bill by the towing company because they needed a special truck to remove it. Stevie got a severe ticking off for inappropriate towing, but he kept his job in the community police. The army tank incident was the talk of the police station and we all had a good laugh about it.

When Stevie and I were on the beat we were called to a lot of housebreakings, particularly in Glasgow's unique tenement flats, most of them built at the end of the nineteenth century or the beginning of the twentieth. These are solid red-stone blocks, usually four storeys high. Narrow lanes separate the backs of the tenements, and this is where the bins are put out.

These days Bohemian types snap up the flats, but there are still quite a few which are sublet to students. The students would often call us after break-ins but not be able to tell us exactly what had been taken because they lived in such chaos anyway that they often couldn't find their belongings even when they hadn't been stolen.

We were also frequently called out to the tenements by women who were being flashed at by men who stood in the lanes outside their back windows. There was no pattern to when the flashers exposed themselves; it was whenever they had an audience, although there would often be a flurry of sightings reported over a period of a few days.

Once I was given the job of standing washing dishes in a woman's house for hours on end, waiting for one of these men to appear and flash at me. There was an unmarked car waiting round the corner to pick the culprit up if he was caught in flagrante. The flasher obviously didn't like the look of me because he never performed while I was stationed at a window. I waited there for hours with my feet going numb pretending to wash dishes while the woman of the house put her feet up and watched *Coronation Street*. Because I never caught anyone it was one of the most tedious jobs I had to do. I stood at the sink for three- or four-hour stretches when all I wanted to do was to get out on the streets and catch criminals.

As I became more confident about the job I learnt lots of different ways to seek out evidence and knew when to write off crimes because there was no evidence to follow up on. One thing that mattered a lot to me was to do my best for people who were victims of crime. It would have been easy to write off some of the more minor crimes, but I felt I owed it to the victims to get justice for them. When a woman who was almost blind was followed home after she came out of a jewellery shop and then robbed of her handbag, I pulled out all the stops to catch the thief. Because of her poor sight she had problems identifying him, but I managed to get enough footage of him from various CCTV cameras to secure a conviction.

A few months after I'd started work as a community police officer I was called to deal with a group of youths who were persecuting an elderly disabled man who was confined to his ground-floor flat. Every night they banged on his window, shouted abuse and generally tormented him. He had endured this for a long time before reporting it to his landlords, a housing association. Staff there passed the information on to me. I made a point of patrolling outside his flat every night the following week with three other community officers. At first I gave the youths a warning, and when they persisted I arrested them for causing a breach of the peace. After several evenings spending a couple of hours locked in a cell at Williamstone police station their antisocial behaviour stopped. One of the housing association officers told me I was getting a reputation for sorting out local problems. I flushed with pleasure. At times like that I felt really good about my job.

I loved to feel that I'd been responsible for preventing a crime. Once I surprised a man trying to break into a car, but before I could arrest him he sprinted off into Kelvingrove Park. I chased him and was running so fast that I thought my lungs were going to burst, but I could see that he was getting away from me. There was a group of Territorial Army guys running through the park and I shouted to one of them, 'Grab him, grab him.' A couple of them tackled him and held on to him until I arrived, handcuffed him and took him back to the station.

I boasted that I'd caught him single-handed, and that hurt his pride – 'Ah wisnae caught by any girl. It was a bunch of guys who stopped me.'

'Don't be daft,' I grinned. 'It was me who caught you.'

I particularly despised crimes against children or elderly people, especially incidents where old people were conned out of their money by bogus workmen. One old lady called Agnes had been tricked twice by the same man. I made a point of visiting her whenever I had a spare ten minutes. I always took round a packet of custard creams and shared a cup of tea with her.

She was a small woman, with grey permed hair and glasses, and her wrinkled face always lit up when I knocked on the door. Her husband had died a few years before and she loved having company.

'So how's your family, hen?' she asked once she'd got me sat down on the sofa with a steaming mug of tea in my hand.

'I've not seen much of them recently, Agnes. I've been so busy at work.'

'Your family's important, hen. Make sure you get up to see them, you never know how much time you've got.'

She loved watching *Countdown* and always encouraged me to sit and watch it with her. The cheesy jokes made her laugh and she was delighted when she got some of the sums right. My dad loved crossword puzzles and had passed the bug on to me, so I often sat and helped her with clues she couldn't get. Agnes was a lovely woman, but no matter what I told her she was so trusting that she carried on opening her door to anyone and everyone.

Another old woman was woken in the middle of the night by a man standing over her bed. She screamed so loud that she scared him off, but was still shaking when I arrived. I was horrified about what might have happened, knowing full well that she could have been raped or murdered. The intruder was never caught because there was no evidence, something I found very frustrating, both for her and for other people he might have gone on to attack.

There was one case where lack of evidence wasn't an issue

but we still didn't have enough to secure a conviction. Stevie
and I had been given a police van to patrol in because it was
Saturday night in July and the west end was buzzing. As we
drove up Byers Road our eyes were peeled for trouble. There
was a good-humoured atmosphere; the students had just
started their summer break and had money to burn.

We were driving up University Avenue when suddenly a
young man ran into the road in front of us and frantically
waved us down. His face was covered in blood, as was the
white shirt he was wearing. We both jumped out of the van to
make sure that he was OK.

'Ah've been attacked,' he cried.

'Are you OK?' I asked. 'What happened? Did you see who
did it?'

'It was five guys who just jumped me and started hitting
me over the head with bottles. They ran down there,' he said,
pointing down the road.

'D'you think you'd be able to identify them?' asked Stevie.

'Ay.'

'What's your name?'

'Darren Betts.'

'Right. Jump in the van, Darren. We'll take you on a tour
of the area to see if you can see them.'

Although he was bleeding heavily, his injuries weren't life-
threatening and he was keen to help the police to catch his
attackers. We drove a couple of hundred yards down the hill
and suddenly Darren shouted, 'That's them,' pointing to five
young men who were walking away from the area. Both Stevie
and I jumped out of the van again and stopped the men. They
were all in their mid-twenties and were dressed alike in shirts

and jeans. We radioed for assistance and asked them where they'd been. They told us they'd been on a night out and were just on their way home. All of them denied having anything to do with the attack on Darren.

Our objective was to get them back to the police office, where they could be questioned and forensic evidence taken. I felt certain they were lying because there were bloodstains on their shirts and grazes on some of their knuckles. I was keen to check the CCTV footage, but couldn't do that until we'd got them back to the station. Another police car arrived to help us and escorted Darren to the nearest hospital to be treated for a head injury. We placed the five men in the back of the police van and they were held at the police station for six hours. During that time we got a full statement from Darren and secured enough CCTV evidence to charge all five with assault.

A year later we went to court. Each of the five accused had his own lawyer. When you give evidence you have to say you can identify the accused, but it was almost impossible to remember who was who. Miraculously I'd written a description of each and managed to identify them correctly in the witness box.

Just when I thought things were going well, one of the defence lawyers turned on me during cross-examination and asked if I'd heard of contamination. I racked my brains trying to think about what he was driving at because I'd prepared well for the case. He proceeded to rip me to shreds because we had placed the five accused in the same van as the witness. He claimed it was possible this was how Darren's blood had got on to their clothes, and that the accused hadn't even been present during the assault.

I knew this wasn't true because there was no way the amount of blood on the witness's head could have found its way on to five shirts and five pairs of hands just by sitting in the same van. I felt more and more frustrated and appalled as I stood in the witness box and realized that even though I knew the men were guilty this clever man had found a loophole. All five were acquitted and it riled me that justice hadn't been done even though there'd been clear evidence linking the five men to the crime.

My priority when Darren flagged us down was to waste no time in tracking down the culprits. The ramifications of how this would play out in the courtroom hadn't crossed my mind. I would have felt I'd let him down if I hadn't tried to locate his attackers straight away. This incident taught me that you can never be totally prepared for giving evidence in court.

In fact we had very little training on this aspect of our jobs. Effectively we were all thrown in at the deep end. No matter how experienced an officer was, I didn't know anyone who wasn't nervous about giving evidence. The worst were the senior officers who had got out of practice after years in their comfy desk jobs. Now and again they'd be unlucky enough to witness a crime and be forced to intervene, and we'd all enjoy watching them doing their utmost to avoid the inevitable court appearance.

It was often exhausting preparing for court because trials had a nasty habit of coinciding with night shifts. At times like that I prayed that cases wouldn't go ahead, because I was too tired to concentrate.

The whole court system is a minefield. It wasn't uncommon to hang around in the corridor outside the courtroom for a week without being called to give evidence. The court staff never bothered to tell us what was happening with cases we were involved in, and the goings-on behind the scenes were a mystery to most of us.

People assume that a courthouse is where justice is done, but often nothing could be further from the truth. There's a great deal of bad practice and sheer incompetence in the system. Files of evidence get lost and there's a lack of communication between police and prosecutors. Sometimes trials are cancelled for the flimsiest of reasons and never get rescheduled because they have to be held within a certain time limit.

Giving evidence in court wasn't a part of the job I enjoyed. I felt it often wasted far too much time and wished the courts could come up with a way of dealing with cases more efficiently. I locked the same people up over and over again because the courts weren't convicting and sentencing them appropriately.

I much preferred being out on the beat dealing with ordinary and not so ordinary people. The locals were beginning to accept me and would give me tip-offs, particularly about drug-dealers, because they were a plague on their neighbourhoods. I acted on that information and regularly submitted criminal intelligence reports. CID officers who were targeting criminals from my area but didn't have enough information to arrest them often called on me to assist them. I could identify people and provide details of their movements. These officers began asking me to help with their inquiries when they were looking for people in connection with serious crimes such as robbery. Sometimes I went along with them when they made an arrest.

The outcome was that I began to get some experience of

how the CID operated, and although I loved the community police I realized that I wanted to get involved with detecting more major crimes: the work was more challenging and complex. Now that I was comfortable tackling minor crimes I felt I was ready for the next stage of my police career. Some officers were content to remain in their comfort zone but I was keen to extend my knowledge and pick up new ideas: I wanted to become a better officer.

As I spent more and more time thinking about how I could move into the CID I got involved in investigating a spate of housebreakings in my area. By this point I'd been in the community police for two years. The burglaries were all in top-floor or first-floor tenement flats. The perpetrator had been climbing up the back drainpipe and forcing open the windows of the first-floor flats or the communal loft hatch and getting into the top flats by breaking in through the ceiling. There had been about ten crimes of this kind altogether, all of them allocated to different CID officers who weren't communicating with each other. As I took an interest in the crimes in my area I realized there was a pattern and asked for all the crime reports to be given to me so that I could look into them. The CID officers were only too happy to offload them.

I noticed that all of these burglaries were committed at a similar time of day, and were located near the home of a local drug addict called Barry McGraw. My first check was with the prisons to make sure he wasn't locked up at the time of the crimes. I found out he'd been released the day before they began. There was blood left at the scene of one of the crimes from a smashed window and a fingerprint at several others.

I called the lab and flagged up Barry McGraw as a suspect

so they could make a quick comparison with his DNA and fingerprints, already on file from previous crimes. While I waited for the result I asked my sergeant if Stevie and I could spend time in plain clothes to monitor Barry McGraw's movements more closely. It wasn't long before he was caught trying to break into a flat. We were tipped off by a member of the public and Stevie and I rushed over in an unmarked police car. Barry ran but didn't get far, and I arrested him for attempted housebreaking. I asked a CID officer to help me interview him on tape, because I wasn't trained to do that.

Barry McGraw sat across the table from me in the bare, boxlike room, which contained only a table, some chairs and a tape machine. He was a small man with a pale face, sunken eyes and greasy hair. I could see the track marks on his skinny arms. He was shaking because he was withdrawing from heroin.

'Can I get a fag, boss?' he said in a trembling voice.

'Ay, depends what you've got to tell us,' said Frank, the CID officer.

'Will ah get oot?' he asked.

'We'll need to see about that,' said Frank, handing him a cigarette.

Frank began the formalities of the interview, naming those present and giving the time and the date.

I started questioning Barry about the various crimes. All he would say was, 'No comment.' It would have been good to get an admission, but I had enough evidence from witnesses and forensics. I started to charge him.

'Charge number ten: you Barry McGraw did break into the dwelling house at flat one hundred and ten Bellfield Avenue, by forcing open the rear window and did steal three gold bracelets, two gold rings, one video recorder, a microwave oven and a TV,' I said.

'That's bullshit,' he broke in. 'I didn't take the microwave or the TV. They bastards have just claimed on the insurance for that. Not'ing to do wi' me.'

I beamed. He'd just made his admission.

I got a pat on the back from the detective inspector. 'Good work, you'd make a good CID officer,' he said. 'How do you fancy a job in plain clothes? There's a vacancy for a female in the Divisional Crime Resource Unit. It's a good stepping stone into the CID.'

'I'd love to work there,' I told him there and then. I was over the moon. This was what I'd been waiting for.

# *Twelve*

It was 6 am. We flattened ourselves against the outside wall of a block of high-rise flats in Plean Street, Yoker, and slid silently along it. We mustn't be seen from our target's home. One officer stayed outside the block directly underneath the target flat in case the occupants threw their drugs or themselves out of the window. As we entered the foyer of the block another officer stood by the concierge just in case he tipped off our target.

I'd joined the plain-clothes unit known as the Plainers three months ago and was loving every minute of it. The work was fascinating and it was bliss not to have to wear the prim police uniform any longer. We could choose our own clothes, our own hairstyles and our own shoes. I celebrated by chucking out the heavy police shoes and loved the new scope and initiative I had.

The focus of Plainers work was targeting crime hotspots, in particular by making drugs raids and cultivating informants. It was a stepping stone into the CID, although we worked in a different way. Unlike CID officers, Plainers operated as a team and didn't have a specific caseload. There were six male officers and two females in our group. Mick was the most experienced, and the more junior officers like me followed his lead.

We Plainers considered ourselves superior to uniformed officers, who we referred to disparagingly as woodentops. In truth we looked down on them now that we had graduated to breaking down doors at dawn and pulling drugs out of various ingenious hiding places including human orifices. Although *Starsky and Hutch* had been absent from the TV screens for several years it was those fictional cops that we modelled ourselves on.

Six of us crept up the back stairwell of the Plean Street flats. Yoker was a very deprived area where the council housed a lot of drug addicts and people with mental health problems. It was around here that we Plainers seemed to spend a lot of our time. Our target lived on the fifth floor, and so as not to blow our cover if we met anybody in the lift, we took the stairs. It was a nightmare lugging what's called the heavy kitbag, containing gloves, plastic bags, labels and a Rammit, a two-handled tool that looks a bit like a rocket-launcher. By the time I got to the fifth floor I was panting for breath.

There is an art to swinging the heavy Rammit at a front-door lock at the proper angle to make the lock spring open without wrecking the entire front door. Mick took it from me and busted the lock at the first attempt.

'Police,' we shouted, adrenalin pumping and hearts racing. The occupants had obviously been sleeping, but there was a sudden burst of activity – everyone jumping out of bed and running around, desperately to find and dispose of their drugs.

We were all squashed into the tiny hallway. It was chaos. A scraggy Alsatian dog lunged at the officer in front of me.

'Get that fucking dog away from me,' he shouted, then grabbed me from behind and used me as a human shield. He was six foot four and built like a tank, yet he was cowering. 'What a wimp,' I thought to myself.

Often dealers have vicious dogs trained to attack anyone their owner doesn't like the look of, and this raid was no exception. I was lucky that the dog didn't go for me.

I spotted one pale skinny man I knew as Billy Hunt, thirty-three years old, with matted brown hair. It was his flat, he was our main target, and I grabbed him. He was hurrying to tip a brown powder that I presumed was heroin down the sink.

'Don't bother trying to get rid of it, Billy,' I said.

Mick grabbed another equally skinny man, Billy's right-hand man Joe Briggs, who was dressed only in his boxer shorts. He had swallowed some drugs and Mick had him in a choke hold.

We seized the usual paraphernalia dealers have – a set of scales, clingfilm and newspaper torn into squares.

As officers pulled the place apart, I looked around the flat and was appalled by the squalor. Used needles and condoms crunched and squelched underfoot. The beds had bare, blood-soaked mattresses on them, and rotting, half-eaten Chinese takeaway food cartons were piled up on a low table. The whole place stank of dog faeces and unwashed bodies. I felt filthy just being there. My skin itched and I wished I didn't have to put my feet on the ground. Just breathing in the same foul air as these people made me scared I might catch something nasty.

A dishevelled young woman in her early twenties appeared from one of the bedrooms. It was Carol Nelson, Billy's girlfriend. She had long, brown, greasy hair, was dressed in a stained nightshirt and was holding a grizzling baby. I could see that her arms were scarred with track marks.

'Get out of ma hoose,' she said weakly, desperately dragging on a cigarette. 'You better have a fucking warrant.'

'Just fucking shut up and listen. Of course we've got a fucking warrant,' said one of the officers.

There was a knock at the door. One of my colleagues opened it and a young woman dressed in jeans and a sweater was escorted into the living room. I noticed at once that she didn't have the same wasted appearance as the others.

'Carol, what the fuck's going on? You promised me you'd stop all this. You're gonna lose your fucking weans.'

She took the baby off Carol, then she turned to one of the police officers, shaking her head.

'My sister promised me she was going to get clean,' she said. She walked over to one of the hall cupboards and opened it to reveal a toddler sleeping soundly in a tiny bed in there. There was a single, naked light bulb swinging from the ceiling and no window. The poor boy's bedroom was about half the size of a police cell. I made a mental note to get in touch with social services about the conditions the children were living in.

'Can I take ma niece and nephew to ma house? I don't want them to see this,' she asked me.

I felt sorry for her and for the children, but before I had a chance to answer a male officer grabbed her roughly and insisted that I search her first, even though it was obvious that she wasn't involved. Her appearance was different, so was her manner and she didn't seem to be under the influence of any drug.

But I'd long ago realized that a lot of police officers passed judgement on the families of drug-users and treated them no differently from the users themselves. I knew that the police who called at our house when my brother James got into trouble would have judged us the same way. He had been a drug-user, and because of my family's experience of drug addiction I viewed this situation differently from my colleagues and was respectful to the families involved. I understood that it wasn't their fault, just as I understood that addiction is not the crime of the century but something that some people are more at risk of falling into than others because of a combination of circumstances that are often out of their control. I tried my best to treat addicts and their families as individuals, understanding how difficult it was to see loved ones fall so hard that they'd do anything to feed their habit, including stealing from their own family.

After the initial uproar the situation in the flat was growing calmer. A lot of the aggression we'd burst in with was spent now that we'd found the evidence we needed of the presence of drugs. The dealers in here were neither as smart nor as desperate as some we knew. One dealer placed a wire under the door mat outside his flat that turned on a light inside whenever anyone stepped on it. It warned him that someone was approaching so that he could quickly dispose of drugs if he needed to.

People would do anything to avoid a bust. Some dealers even stationed lookouts across the road from the police office. They watched our movements and came to recognize unmarked cars. When they saw them leaving in convoy, usually heading out to the west of the city on a drugs raid, a phone call would be made and the drugs would be moved before we even reached the roundabout at the end of the road. In some ways they were far cleverer than we were, and it was quite rare for us to catch one of the big dealers, the linchpins in the smuggling operations. It was far easier to pick up the people at the bottom of the dealing chain, who were often users themselves. Even under interrogation they would never spill the names or details of the Mr Bigs. These were hardcore gangsters, and a lot more frightening than we were. A lengthy jail sentence was a better option than floating down the Clyde with your throat slit.

Our division's oldest dealer was a grandmother called Maggie Stewart. She'd been dealing for years, and when the council wanted to demolish all the blocks of flats in her street she refused point-blank to move and continued to deal surrounded by derelict houses. Dealing had been passed down through the generations of her family. She liked the fact that her flat was on the top floor, giving her 360-degree vision of any approaching police cars. She sold to anyone, though, including undercover police officers, and time and time again that was her downfall. She'd been convicted and jailed more times than she could count.

We strutted around the flat like peacocks, full of bravado and self-congratulation. The drug-users there were shaking uncontrollably with fear from the beginnings of withdrawal from the heroin they depended on. They knew they were about to be charged with dealing and that if they were convicted they were looking at a long stretch in jail. Billy sat in his dirty vest, his head in his hands, saying over and over again under his breath, 'Fucking hell, fucking hell.'

Billy, Joe, Carol and her sister Joan were taken into two separate rooms to be searched.

Billy started shouting at the male officer who was searching him, 'Leave me alone, I've got witnesses. Carol, Carol, can you hear this?'

'What youz fucking doing to ma man?' shouted Carol from the other room where I was searching her. 'Ah want ma lawyer. I'm making a complaint about you.'

'Do it. We're the biggest gang in the world,' shouted one of the officers.

Somebody knocked on the door. One of the officers ran to answer it and pulled in a hapless junkie who'd come round hoping to score. We arrested him too. Sometimes people like him who got caught up in raids would give evidence for the prosecution if we dropped charges against them.

We let Joan take the kids away, and hauled everyone else down to the police station.

'If I gie you a turn will you let me out?' whined Billy. I could see he was badly strung out. He obviously couldn't care less about Carol and his kids.

'Depends what it is,' said Mick, unimpressed.

'You need to go right now to flat 53 in our block. There's kit in there.'

He gave us more details and we organized who was going to go down there and raid the flat.

'Are we going to ask one of the woodentops to help us?' I asked Mick.

'Ay, but we'll need to keep them right,' he said.

'We can keep them in the car for back-up because they'd probably fuck up something like this,' I said. I strode into the TV room, where some young uniformed officers were on their break.

'Are youz available to help us out with a turn?' I said, speaking fast and confidently. Both nodded eagerly.

'We'll just ask the sergeant if we can get away,' one of them replied.

'No bother, I've done that already. The sergeant is fine about it.'

'Who is it we're going to?' asked the officer.

'It's the Fletcher family,' I said knowingly, lording it over them with my superior knowledge of Glasgow's criminal families. I'd forgotten my own discomfort as a uniformed officer when Plainers had treated me that way. Both the officers gave me a blank look. They'd never heard of the Fletcher family.

As I walked out of the room I heard one of them whisper to the other, 'What an arsehole.'

I was so full of self-importance that I looked down on them for not knowing who the Fletcher family were. I'd bought into the Plainers culture so completely that I couldn't see what was happening to me.

There was a suspicion that there might be weapons in the house, so we had to get a senior officer's permission to call out the Armed Response Unit for back-up. When this had been done we rushed down to the address. It was a good result. We seized four nine-ounce bars of cannabis which had not yet been cut up, but no weapons.

By the end of the shift six people had been charged with drugs offences. We all slapped each other on the back and hailed our magnificent police work.

Although we were on a high I kept thinking about young girls like Carol, who got pregnant at the age of sixteen or seventeen and were given a house by the council. I guessed that she'd been hit on by a young dealer who wooed her, moved in with her and used the flat to sell drugs from. Or maybe she'd started using drugs at a young age herself, and the two of them together had set up a little dealing business.

A lot of the dealers we pulled in were small-timers who were just selling enough to support their own habits. Society had failed them and I wasn't sure how locking them in police cells was going to help them or anyone else. Sometimes they died in the cells because they'd swallowed all their drugs when we arrived.

I wondered what the future held for the two children we'd found on the raid. The vicious circle would probably continue. Either they'd stay with their junkie parents or they'd be taken into care, where their upbringing wouldn't be much better.

I tried to push these gloomy thoughts away. After our long but successful shift we began celebrating in the usual way – we locked the door of one of the offices in the police station and got out the whisky. A heavy drinking session began as we relived the operation moment by moment. There was a lot of camaraderie and a lot of in jokes.

'That was some result,' an officer called Paul said.

'Ay, but youz left me with Joe. I was trying to stop him swallowing the drugs and the bastard bit my hand,' said Mick accusingly.

'I don't know what you're talking about,' said Paul. 'When I came in you were choking him.'

'Ay, ah know, but that was because he was biting me while you were prancing aboot with the drugs, ya fucker. Have you done the note yet? Those CID bastards cannae slag us now with a result like that.'

'That hoose was minging,' I said. 'Did you see the amount of needles and condoms all over the place?'

'Ay, better get checked out for HIV,' said Mick. Everybody roared with laughter.

Then we started slagging each other off drunkenly. If anyone wanted to go to the toilet the door was locked behind them to preserve our secret drinking den. I often spent four or five hours after my shift in these sessions, sometimes the whole night. And in the morning we crept home with the empty whisky bottles concealed in black bags.

I started to go on police nights out which also involved heavy drinking, happy to be part of the team. I'd been in the police for seven years now, I was twenty-eight and I'd reached a point where I was playing the game. I'd lost my independent streak and was more willing to swallow the 'We're the biggest gang in the world' mentality. I was ambitious, and getting into the CID had become very important to me. It was touted as the ultimate in police work, and because I was longing to work there I was uncritically buying into police culture. Just as we Plainers looked down on the woodentops, CID officers looked down on us. I saw the Plainers as a stopgap and couldn't wait to move on.

Knowledge was power. Because we knew more than less experienced officers we revelled in parading our superior knowledge and despised those we now saw as beneath us, most of all the woodentops. Rubbing in our superior rank at every opportunity inflated our own sense of importance. This was a vein that ran all the way through the police. I'd run into it at the beginning of my training at Tulliallan when the sergeants boasted about their greater knowledge of criminals and how to tackle them. The very same attitude afflicted those senior officers who treated us like dirt in our turn because their greater knowledge and experience gave them power over us and our careers. I didn't know it at the time, but during this period I'd lost myself. I'd succumbed hook, line and sinker to the police brainwashing process.

I was often dispatched on intelligence-gathering operations to the homes of suspected drug-dealers and others believed to be misbehaving. Sometimes I pretended to be selling catalogues and was quite proud of myself for what I felt was a very convincing performance.

One day I was sitting in the office nursing a hangover when the phone rang. My head was pounding but I was getting used to that – I'd been drinking heavily with my colleagues for more than a year. The boozing sessions helped us all unwind, and we always kept a bottle of spirits in our drawer. There was a big raid planned for that evening so I knew that afterwards we'd be drinking again.

The woman on the phone sounded scared. She'd told the

duty sergeant that she had some information and had been put through to us.

At first all I could hear was the sound of sobbing.

'I can't help you unless you talk to me,' I said gently.

'He'll kill me if he knows I've called you,' she whispered. Then she hung up.

The call worried me because the woman's distress sounded genuine. She started to call me regularly, and eventually she told me that she was being controlled by a violent man who forced her and another woman to work as prostitutes in a flat near the police office. She only gave me a first name – Joanne – and I assumed it wasn't her real name. After a lot of coaxing she told me her tormentor's name – Colin Wandsworth. I checked him out and found he was known to us and had been a suspect in several cases where prostitutes had been attacked and in one case murdered. On his computer record there were flashing signs warning officers to approach him with caution because he was violent and carried weapons. We'd never managed to pin anything on him because the prostitutes were always too scared to testify. It all tied in with Joanne's story. I'd never dealt with Wandsworth personally but I'd heard that he often made complaints and carried a tape recorder with him hoping to collect evidence against us.

Joanne had cause to be terrified and I was worried about her safety. After she'd been calling me for a month she gave me the address of the flat where she and the other woman were forced to work. She told me that Wandsworth was due back at noon, that he'd be bringing men with him for them to have sex with and that he beat them up if they refused. I was in the office by myself because everyone else was at court so I asked the uniformed sergeant on the shift if some officers could go round there and investigate. He wouldn't hear of it.

'No, my officers are down to do a football match later so I can't give you any. Fuck her anyway, she's just a prostitute, fucking waste of space.'

'With all due respect, do you not think that somebody's life is more important than the football?'

'Football comes first. We need the numbers.'

He saw the look of horror on my face. Although I'd got involved in the macho culture because I wanted a job in CID, I wasn't prepared to go along with attitudes like that.

'That's just the way we do things here,' he said, and walked away before I could say anything else, leaving me open-mouthed.

Joanne stopped calling me, the flat was closed down and I never heard from her again. I felt that she had relied on me to help her but I'd let her down. I'd worked hard to build up her trust and she had put herself at risk by giving me Wandsworth's name and the address of the flat. Because there was no one available to raid the flat we'd missed a golden opportunity to get vital evidence against a man we knew was dangerous, leaving him free to carry on persecuting women like Joanne.

One of the more unpleasant jobs I had to do as a Plainer was to watch lots of porn films to look for evidence of children being used for sex in them. We had a tip-off that a particular chain of video shops was selling child porn films and seized more than 1,000 videos. We raided all three shops in the chain and to save time we concentrated on watching the films that had been stashed under the counter and were not on open display. We had detained the shop owner, but because in Scotland police can only hold a suspect for six hours before questioning him or her, it was a race against time to try to find some evidence.

We all huddled round a small TV screen. 'Who's bringing the popcorn in?' joked one officer.

A lot of the films showed 'shemales' – people with female breasts and penises. At first there was plenty of banter about 'giving her one' and one of the officers joked that one of the shemales looked like an effeminate male officer on the shift. Then most of us got bored and kept glancing at the screen while we were writing up our notes. But worryingly one officer remained glued to the screen with an animated expression on his face. Soon after that he was moved to another department for demanding sexual favours from a prostitute.

Although we waited as long as we could, by the time Mick and I interviewed the video shop owner we still hadn't found any child porn. Mick switched on the tape recorder for the interview and cleared his throat. The owner, a small, hairy, sweaty man, looked nervous.

'So, Mr Bryant, this morning myself and my colleagues came to all three of your premises and seized a number of videos. Is that correct?'

Bryant nodded.

'I'm going to select one of them at random and I'd like you to tell me about it please.'

He picked up a video out of a pile he had brought into the interviewing room and glanced at the title.

'*Greedy Cunt*. Could you tell us what's in the film?' asked Mick. We both turned to each other and tried not to laugh.

Bryant was forthcoming in the interview about the adult entertainment he sold, perfectly legally, and we never found any evidence that he was selling child porn. In the end he was released without charge.

# Thirteen

I was lying in bed one Sunday morning in my flat in Glasgow trying to open my eyes. It was my day off but I'd been on a police night out on Saturday and now I had a splitting headache, as well as feeling bloated from the amount of alcohol I'd been drinking lately. I'd got home at about 4 am after moving from the pub to a nightclub popular with both police and criminals. I felt as if I was never away from the police these days, because I worked such long hours and often did overtime. When I did finally get off duty I'd still meet up with my colleagues in the evening at a pub or club. Our group of eight Plainers was very tight-knit. The nature of what we were dealing with made us very close and we were happy to be in each other's company all the time.

The phone rang and I held my hands up to my head to stop the noise.

'Hello,' I croaked.

'Hi Anne, it's Julie. What's wrong with you? You sound terrible.'

'Oh, I was out again last night,' I groaned. 'It was my third night out this week. I don't think I can drink any more.'

'I'm the same, I've been out four nights this week. In fact this morning is the first time for ages I haven't woken up with a hangover. Should I call you back when you're feeling more human?'

'No, it's OK, we haven't chatted for ages. What have you been up to?'

'I'm getting moved to the Female and Child Unit.'

The Female and Child Unit dealt predominantly with rape and sex offences against children and the police were always looking for female officers to work there. Julie and I had done enough years of service to be selected for that department. I was worried about her going there because when we'd first joined the police she had hinted that something had happened to her as a child and I had a feeling that she must have been abused. She'd never elaborated and I didn't push it, but I hoped she'd be able to cope with such traumatic work.

'How d'you feel about that?' I asked her. 'I've been asked to move there but I don't want to deal with that kind of crime. I'm still with the Plainers. That's me there for two years now. I'm trying to get into CID.'

'The Plainers sounds good. I don't want to go to the Female and Child Unit,' she said. 'But they're telling me it will be a good career move for me, so I don't feel I've got much of a choice about it. I've been speaking to the girl I'm replacing; she's been doing it for three years. She told me that when she got a phone call from a ten-year-old girl telling her that her uncle had been touching her and thought to herself "Is that all?", she knew then it was time to get out.'

'That's terrible,' I said. 'That's why I don't want to do it. But even though I'm not in the Female and Child Unit I've been dealing with a lot of that kind of thing. I've been taking a lot of DNA samples for sex crimes. You'll probably end up doing that.

'There's quite a big case going on in Edinburgh involving a judge's daughter who got raped. The same guy turned up here. He was spying on a young girl getting changed in her bedroom in a basement flat and he left some of his saliva on the window. We managed to get DNA from that, so now we're looking for the guy, but he's not on the file. I've been going round taking fresh DNA from known sex offenders who aren't on the database.'

I told Julie that I'd visited one guy who looked like a typical paedophile, with his bulbous nose, greasy hair, and thick-framed glasses. He was wearing a sweaty vest and his house was swarming with flies.

'When he opened his door I introduced myself and said, "There's been a crime of indecency. Could you give us your DNA?"' At the time police officers could only take DNA samples with permission from the suspect.

'He said to me, 'Is it a wee girl?' I was totally shocked because it was a wee girl and I told him it was. Then he said, "No, it wasn't me. I only do wee boys."'

'God, sick bastard,' sighed Julie.

'Ah know. I'm fed up with sex offenders, but one of the inquiries I went on was in a dungeon and it was really funny. There were two women who worked as dominatrixes. They had guys who went to see them who liked to dress up as babies. It was hilarious, they were telling me all sorts of stories about the men liking to lick their shoes. But they didn't have sex with the men, it wasn't part of their job. They get paid lots of money to have male slaves. It sounds like the perfect job.'

We both laughed.

'Oh, by the way, did you hear about Clare? Do you remember Paul, her partner? He went into CID. Well he left his wife and two kids for her and she's left her husband for him. They're living together now.'

'God, I haven't spoken to her for years, but I'm no surprised. It seems like just about everyone's on their second marriage. This job's enough to put you off getting married, it's full of drunks and womanizers.'

'My head's banging, Julie. Why don't I call you tomorrow and we can sort out meeting up so we can catch up properly?'

'No bother, it would be good to get together soon,' said Julie.

I lay in bed rubbing my pounding head and suddenly remembered I'd arranged to meet my mum in town in half an hour, so I threw on some clothes and staggered off to face the day – I made it just in time. We decided to have a cup of tea, and as we stood on the glass-sided escalator going up to a cafe in a shopping mall I noticed Mum's bag was casually hanging from her shoulder. A man was standing quite close to her.

'Mum, keep hold of your bag or someone'll steal it,' I said sharply to her. I was so used to dealing with crimes where someone had run up to an unsuspecting woman, snatched her handbag and then run away. Then I said under my breath, 'I don't like the look of that guy.'

'For God's sake, Anne, you're not at work now.' My mum wasn't used to seeing me so on edge. All the same, when we went into the cafe and ordered two cups of tea, she still put her bag down on the floor.

'Mum, do you want your bag stolen?'

'What's wrong with you, Anne? I can't see any thieves!'

'It only takes a minute for someone to steal your bag, Mum. I don't like the look of him over there.'

'I'll go and dangle my bag in his face and see if he wants it, will I?' She laughed, but I didn't laugh back. Instead I glared at her. Mum looked concerned at my reaction.

'Are you stupid? Your bag's lying open, Mum.'

'Don't you dare speak to me like that! You're not at your work now. I don't like the person you're turning into.'

'Just do as you're told,' I said bossily.

'For God's sake listen to the way you're speaking to me. The whole family's noticed the way you're behaving, as if you're at work and we're all criminals or half-stupid. You're like a robot. You don't seem to care about anything or anyone any more.'

I gave her a blank look. 'What are you on about?' I asked.

To my horror I saw tears welling up in her eyes. 'What's happened to you?'

I went quiet and felt guilty. We didn't speak for a few minutes while I thought about what she'd just said, and the more I thought the more I knew that she was right. I didn't like the person I was turning into, but I'd been trying not to think about it, or even to admit there was something to think about. Before I joined the police I'd been completely carefree. I was sensitive to others and always put my family first. When I used to go to clubs I never thought twice about leaving my bag at a table while I went off to have a dance. At parties where I hardly knew anyone I paid no heed at all to things like that. I was much more innocent in those days, trusted people and didn't judge them the way I was doing now, even members of my own family. I was developing an 'I know best' attitude, and if anyone did dare to criticize me I just brushed them and their comments aside.

I used to have such a laugh with my mum. When I came in from a night out with my friends, I would call her and regale her with stories about what went on, who I'd met, things I'd said and heard.

I burned with shame. What my mum thought mattered far more to me than what the police thought, and I realized that she was talking a lot of sense. It wasn't till I'd really upset her that I started to wake up to what I'd become. The life I was leading had transformed me into an intolerant and arrogant person, someone I didn't like at all. It was at that point, sitting there in the cafe with my mum weeping opposite me, that I vowed to change. But there was one thing I couldn't change. I'd lost my innocence, and nothing I could do would bring it back. I turned to my mum and put my arms round her.

'I'm sorry,' I said, tears rolling down my cheeks.

# *Fourteen*

'Come in, Anne. Close the door,' said Detective Chief Inspector Brenda Ross briskly.

I'd been summoned to see her at the divisional police headquarters and walked warily into her boxlike office. It was smarter than most offices at the police station, with framed prints of police awards on the walls and fancy chairs. DCI Ross was a large, heavyset woman in her late forties, with hair gone prematurely white. She was dressed in a cheap, sensible polyester suit with a white blouse underneath. She sat very straight in a big swivel chair and gestured for me to sit down in the smaller one across the desk from her.

'A typical way for someone in authority in the police to make more junior officers feel small,' I thought to myself as I sat down. I had no idea why she wanted to see me and could only hope that I hadn't done something wrong that I wasn't even aware of.

'Have you heard about the murder of Margo Lafferty?' she asked, skipping pleasantries and getting straight to the point.

I nodded. 'I've heard a bit through the grapevine and seen the stuff in the papers.'

'There's an inquiry team up and running,' she said.

Margo was a 27-year-old prostitute whose naked body had been found in West Regent Street Lane on 28 February 1998. She'd been battered and strangled.

'I knew Margo well,' she said, sighing. 'I know a lot of the girls well. I've done some work down at Base 75, the prostitutes' drop-in. We've got DNA from the scene and I'm following some leads, but I've got a really important job that I'd like you to take on.

'It's coming up to a week since Margo was murdered, and what I want you to do is go to the lab and look at the clothes she was wearing when she died, then go out and buy some stuff as similar as possible to hers. You're Margo's double, so I'm gonnae get you dressed as Margo and walking where she walked with a view to catching the guy who did it. Let's see if he comes back this week. We've got *Crimewatch* involved. I've heard you're keen to get into CID and I'm sure doing this will help your career.'

She explained that there were two reasons for doing the reconstruction. The first was to jog the memories of potential witnesses who'd been in the area when the murder was committed. The second was to get information from the punters who used prostitutes close to where the murder took place to find out if they'd been involved.

We didn't have a description of the suspect, but with luck that would change after the reconstruction.

I sat looking at the DCI, not sure what to think. Clearly she was giving me an order, not an option. And I wasn't overjoyed that she thought I was the double of a junkie who walked the streets to feed her habit. I didn't know what she had in mind, but it wouldn't be the same as posing as a housewife washing up at the kitchen window, waiting for a flasher who never appeared.

As DCI Ross had instructed, I went to the forensic lab and looked at Margo's clothes. I shivered as I held the crumpled garments. She'd been found with her clothes beside her, and I wondered if they'd been forced off her before or after she was killed. She'd had on a bright turquoise crocheted crop top with matching trousers. The clothes looked tiny and would have fitted a girl of twelve or thirteen.

'There's no way I'm going to wear anything crocheted or see-through,' I said to myself. 'But I suppose it could have been worse; at least she wasn't wearing a miniskirt and thigh-length boots.'

I had obviously been sorry to hear about the murder, but hadn't thought much more about it. Now that I'd handled Margo's clothes I felt closer to her and queasy about what DCI Ross expected me to do.

I headed into town and hunted high and low for clothes like Margo's, but it was the middle of winter and I couldn't find that summery turquoise shade anywhere. Eventually I went into a cheap shop with a bargain basement with last summer's stuff on offer at knockdown prices and ransacked a huge pile of clothes all bundled together in a big basket.

'Bingo!' I said under my breath. I pulled out a pair of French flared trousers in stretchy turquoise nylon. They were the kind of skin-tight trousers that would give you bulges where you didn't have them before. The trousers cost just £2 and I found a matching, tight, turquoise top for £1, so I had

£47 change from the £50 DCI Ross had given me to hand back to her.

I had very little time to prepare. All I knew was that I had to go to police headquarters, where there was going to be a press conference. DCI Ross said she'd collect me from the local police office beforehand. It was as I was getting changed into the gaudy clothes I'd bought that Tommy, one of my colleagues, popped his head round the door and managed to leer and look scornful at the same time as he joked about how much business I'd get tonight.

'Fuck off, you fat bastard. Get out of the ladies' changing room,' I said, throwing a rolled-up pair of socks at him. He wasn't involved in the case, but he thought it was hilarious that I was having to get dressed up as a prostitute.

I was starting to feel uncomfortable as the reality of what I was about to do hit me. Wearing clothes like the ones Margo had worn was very unnerving. I wondered how Margo had felt as she had got ready to go out on to the streets for the last time. Had she had any sense of what was waiting for her out there? The only difference between us at this moment was that I wasn't taking drugs to dull the emotional pain of my life in the way that she had done.

Time to get started. I shut my locker, gave one last longing look at my thick woolly jumper and parka coat hanging up there, then walked out of the changing room and headed into the street.

DCI Ross was sitting in a standard issue CID Peugeot waiting for me with the engine running. 'Oh you look good,' she said admiringly, as she checked me over from top to toe. I didn't answer, feeling resentful that she'd put me in this position. It wasn't her who was going to have to walk the streets in skimpy clothing on a freezing-cold winter night pretending to be a dead prostitute. She briefed me about the press conference and told me she'd do all the talking.

She parked the car outside Strathclyde Police headquarters in Glasgow city centre. It was referred to as coward's castle because that was where many of the senior officers spent their days, avoiding any hands-on involvement in crime, instead making decisions that affected frontline officers' careers.

As she jumped out I saw that she'd managed to tuck her skirt and signature trench coat into her knickers and had everything on show. I followed her into the lift and wrestled with my conscience about telling her. Her humiliation would pay her back for the way she'd made me dress up as a prostitute, and maybe it would take the focus off me if she presented herself to the newshounds like that. But when the lift slowed down my conscience got the better of me and I told her before we made our entrance.

She straightened herself out and then glued a smile onto her face as we walked into the room full of newspaper, radio and TV journalists, most of them men. As DCI Ross began to explain what I'd be doing, one of the journalists called out, 'Does she have a name?' I was introduced as Anne.

'You're all welcome to come out and take photos,' said the DCI. 'We're following a few leads, but I don't want to go into what they are right now.'

'Can we speak to the policewoman?' asked another journalist.

DCI Ross shook her head and wouldn't let me answer any questions. All those male eyes giving me the once-over made me feel quite dirty, as if I'd somehow let myself down. I felt that they were looking at me in exactly the same way they would have looked at Margo, and I felt more and more as if I was becoming her.

The press conference ended and DCI Ross said she'd drop me at the 'drag', the red-light area where Margo had worked.

'Just walk up and down and don't worry about anything. There'll be plain clothes officers stationed nearby,' she said as she parked the car a few yards away.

I shivered in the wind as I made my way towards the drag. I was glad I'd managed to put a pair of tights on underneath my trousers. They were thick, woolly ones but the trousers were so thin that I felt as if all I was wearing was a pair of tights. Some of the girls were standing ahead of me in little huddles and a few were by themselves. I couldn't help feeling anxious because of what had happened to Margo. The patch on Bothwell Street where she usually stood was under a clock tower in an office block that was only used during the day. Girls disappeared into cars. They had struck lucky – or unlucky, depending on how you looked at it. I tried to make a mental note of the car number plates because I was worried about their safety.

I rested my back against the brick wall underneath the huge wall clock. One of the girls who stood close to me was giving me dirty looks. She was shivering with cold, her painfully thin legs barely covered by her miniskirt.

I smiled at her but she glared back. I didn't want to draw too much attention to myself and I certainly didn't want a fight.

'This is ma bit!' she shouted across to me. I noticed that

her two front teeth were missing. Rather than get involved in any trouble I moved away. There was room enough for everybody.

I watched as the same cars drove slowly past me and around the block and back again, waiting to pick up a girl. A black hatchback was heading in my direction. As it got nearer it slowed to a crawl. I could hear rave music thumping through the open windows and could make out two men inside staring at me. Most girls wouldn't go with two men – it was too dodgy. I moved quickly away from the edge of the pavement; I'd heard of girls being snatched.

As I edged back towards the safety of the building walls, the car sped off. I sensed a ball of tension hardening in my stomach, and felt increasingly threatened by the hostility of the girls around me and the potential threat from the punters, any of whom could be Margo's murderer. I wasn't even sure if the police would be able to protect me if anything happened because they were stationed such a distance away. I didn't have a radio so I'd shoved a panic alarm into my pocket – the same type that sexual health projects sometimes hand out free to prostitutes – and was hoping its loud, piercing noise would summon help. But I also knew that the girls relied on each other for protection rather than the police, and I hoped they'd be a safety net for me too.

I paraded back and forth on the pavement. The minutes felt like hours and the cold gnawed deeper and deeper inside me.

'Margo! Margo!'

The screeching female voice seemed to be coming from behind me. I turned to see a girl making her way towards me with outstretched arms. As she reached me I could see the tell-tale glaze of heroin in her eyes.

'Margo, fucking good to see you.'

'I'm not Margo,' I said quietly. 'Margo's dead.'

'You're her double,' she slurred. 'Do you know Margo? She works here.'

'No,' I said. She wasn't listening to me.

'Do you want to come and stand with us?' She gestured towards a group of girls huddled together a bit further down the street.

'It's alright, thanks anyway,' I said and walked away. The whole situation felt surreal. This young woman was so off her face she didn't even know that her friend had been murdered a week before.

I crossed the road and entered a much darker street. This was the route that Margo had taken. There were fewer girls here.

An ordinary-looking man in his mid-thirties approached. He looked the married type.

'Looking for business darlin'?' he asked.

'Oh fuck off,' I said through chattering teeth. I thought he was about to ask me again and I was ready to open my mouth to reply angrily when I realized that this time he wasn't talking to me but to a girl standing next to me. Her name was Frankie; she was Asian and was wearing white plastic Spice Girl boots. She had a hare lip that caused her to speak with a lisp. The two went off together and I carried on walking up and down. I wanted to beg her not to go, but watched her instead as she disappeared down a dark road. The fact that Margo had been murdered just a week before didn't seem to have made the girls more cautious. For them it was business as usual.

The temperature had dropped even further. As it reached 2 am I could hardly feel my feet and had to keep moving to try to stay warm. I headed further up the street. It was darker here with fewer streetlights. I was getting nearer to where Margo had been murdered and felt more and more uneasy. What had her life been like? I wondered. How did she end up in prostitution? Did the job scare her? How did she feel in her final moments?

I recognized the blast of the same loud rave music being played in the distance, and my heart thudded hard as the same black hatchback from earlier sped past me. As I walked towards one of the lanes, my feet felt unsteady on the cobblestones. It was so dark I could hardly see in front of me. Fear climbed from my stomach into my throat. I carried on walking and was blinded all at once by a huge flash of light.

I had walked into a barrage of flashbulbs. The photographers were massed across the street. I was sure I looked like a rabbit caught in headlights.

It was a macabre moment, as I stood right next to the spot where Margo had been murdered. I felt huge pity for her, imagining how terrified she must have been, alone in this dark street with her killer. And yet she'd put up a good fight. As hard as her life must have been, she wasn't ready to let it go.

I stood for about twenty minutes being photographed from all angles, and then was driven back to the station to change my clothes. Not only was I frozen, I felt so mentally and physically exhausted that everything seemed to be happening in slow motion. No one really spoke to me, so I kept my feelings to myself. By the time I stumbled into bed it was 5 am.

The story was splashed across the papers the next day, but I couldn't face looking at myself so I didn't buy any of them. I went into work at 10 am, a couple of hours later than usual, and got lots of jibes about my 'sexy' appearance. Cuttings from various newspapers were thrust into my hands. All of them had splashed my photo across their pages, and some of my colleagues had cheekily blanked out certain words so that it read as if I was the prostitute. It was the usual police banter, always in bad taste, but this time I couldn't laugh off the comments. Spending so many hours walking in Margo's footsteps meant that every joke struck a nerve.

# Fifteen

I was sent to Kingston Road police station on the outskirts of Glasgow city centre while I waited for a place to become vacant in the CID. This was normal practice, as only about three officers were appointed to the CID every six months. I was back in uniform because it didn't make sense to continue in the Plainers and get involved in long-term cases I wouldn't be around to finish.

Our beat covered part of the city centre, including the red-light district. Not much went on during the day, but things livened up after dark.

Ever since that conversation with my mum about how much I'd changed I'd been thinking hard and had decided to drastically reduce my drinking. So rather than celebrate my twenty-ninth birthday by getting drunk with other police officers I chose to spend it with my family.

I seldom joined police nights out now, and was choosy about which ones. Most of the officers I worked with were colleagues rather than close friends, and I was happy to keep things that way. I no longer felt the need to be part of the 'biggest gang in the world'. But I also feared that I was becoming far too cynical about life. Years of exposure to police culture and to criminals had hardened me. Nothing surprised me any more. I observed the bitterness in older police officers and was terrified that I'd end up like them. I missed feeling innocent and carefree more than ever. The job was a weight bearing down on me.

At Kingston Road I wandered into the canteen before my first shift started, to get a cup of tea and chat to my new colleagues. There was a pool table, a dining table, some comfortable chairs and a TV in the room, and in the corner stood a fruit machine we called a puggy.

I smiled, said hello to a couple of people and sat down with my tea. I noticed that the shift seemed to be divided into groups. There was a loud, cocky group of young male officers in their early to mid-twenties who had probably been in the job for four or five years, a tall brunette female officer who was hanging on their every word, and some quiet young female police officers who looked uneasy. The brunette officer, who I found out was called Tracy, had a scratchy voice that grated on me every time she opened her mouth. She was continually bending over the male officers in a provocative way, the kind of woman who made it that much harder for the rest of us to be taken seriously.

Sitting by herself in a corner was a female officer with a pleasant face and short brown hair. Her name was Karen. At the other end of the room a very overweight older constable called Jamie was gorging himself on fish and chips.

I listened to the loud young male officers bragging about some crime they'd cracked and I could tell they had a lot to learn, but the younger female officers seemed impressed, while the older man who was munching seemed happy to let the youngsters brag away, and never mind his years of experience.

'How many tickets did you issue today?' asked one of the young officers.

'Oh no,' I groaned inwardly. 'I can see we're dealing with crimes of the century here, this is going to be fun.'

'Five, two red-lighters,' said one of the others.

'Well I got six,' said the first one proudly.

'Oh, I issued a ticket today,' said Karen quietly. I could tell by her accent that she wasn't from Glasgow. I guessed that she might be from somewhere in the Fife area. The cocky officers glanced at her briefly without acknowledging her remark, then went back to their own conversation. She looked hurt and seemed to retreat into her shell.

The conversation turned to an imminent police night out. The young men asked the other girls if they were going but completely ignored Karen. They started laughing and joking about the last police night out and their plans for their Christmas booze-up, an overnight affair which had already been booked six months ahead. Some of the married officers joked about what fun they'd be having with their wives stuck at home with the kids.

'And you were sitting on someone's knee in your miniskirt at the last police night out,' said Mike, a particularly sleazy-looking young officer, to Tracy. 'Did you have any knickers on?' He was undressing her with his eyes as he asked, something she seemed to welcome.

Then another overweight older constable walked into the canteen and headed towards the one who'd been eating fish and chips.

'I've just been to the Chinky's,' he said.

'Oh you should have told me you were going, Pat, you could have got something for me,' said Jamie.

'You're not allowed to use words like "Chinky" any more,' one of the younger officers grinned, taking a swipe at political correctness. The others roared with laughter. 'Anyway I'm just off down the Paki shop. Anyone want anything?'

Once again everyone roared with laughter, including the sergeants.

Jamie looked round furtively just in case a Chinese or Asian officer suddenly walked into the room.

'So much for treating everyone the same,' I thought to myself. I didn't feel that I'd fit in with this lot at all.

In the briefing room the sergeants paired people up for shifts, and I wondered if they'd put Mike with another female. Like Karen I could see that I wasn't going to fit in with the shift, but unlike her I wasn't just starting out and I knew that I would only be there until a place came up for me in CID.

'Who should I work with?' said Karen timidly when the sergeants failed to pair her up with anyone.

'Oh, you can stay and work at the uniform bar or report-write,' said one of the sergeants dismissively.

I walked into the female locker room to put on my belt and jacket and saw one of the young female officers in there getting changed. She told me that her name was Michelle and that she and the other young woman on the shift, whose name was Susan, had started at the same time.

'How're you enjoying the shift?' Michelle asked.

'Well some of those young male officers seem to be a bit full of themselves,' I said.

'I'm just learning the job, so I try to keep my mouth shut,' she said. I thought she looked tense and anxious.

'If you want any help with anything just let me know,' I said. 'I'm here if you need me. Have you got a regular partner, a tutor cop who's showing you what to do?'

She seemed hesitant, then she said, 'The sergeant keeps pairing me up with Mike, but I'm not learning much on the job with him.'

'Why not?' I asked. 'You should be learning a lot out on the beat.'

She paused again. 'Mike seems more interested in telling me he's not getting on with his wife than in teaching me the job. He keeps phoning me on his days off and it's really pissing my boyfriend off, but I don't know what to do about it.'

'What exactly is he saying to you?' I asked.

'He's got a routine. He started off by telling me that his wife doesnae understand him, then he said that he really enjoys my company and that he could really open up to me.'

'Pass the sick bucket, here we go,' I thought to myself.

'Then he started making excuses to do the night shift with me. Now he parks up, brushes against me and tells me he finds me attractive. And as I said before, he's phoning me on my days off, asking me what I'm up to.'

'Have you tried to talk to anyone about this?'

'No, the sergeant keeps pairing me up with him.'

'Look, don't worry, I'll do what I can to help you,' I said. 'You can talk to me about this any time, you don't need to put up with it.' I was alarmed at what I'd heard, but not surprised. I had come across other young women officers who had experienced the same problems.

I was determined to do what I could to help Michelle. I knew the sergeants were colluding with Mike's behaviour and were quite happy to keep pairing him with young women. I decided that eventually I would be working with him and that I'd confront him then. But I never did get paired up with him, so despite my good intentions I wasn't able to confront Mike on her behalf.

Because I noticed that Karen was still painfully isolated from the rest of the shift, I made a point of asking the sergeant to be paired up with her whenever I could. She seemed grateful to have someone to work with and was eager to learn.

'All I want is to be a good police officer,' she said. 'But nobody wants to work with me. I'm not as popular as the other girls and I don't really seem to fit in.'

'I noticed you were sitting on your own,' I said.

'That's normal,' she replied. 'The others bitch about me behind my back. They think I'm a waste of space and refuse to work with me.'

'Have you done many cases?'

She shook her head. All she'd done was hand out a few parking tickets and deal with a couple of breach-of-the-peace cases. I vowed to myself there and then that I was going to show her how to arrest a real criminal.

The next time we were on night shift together I decided that we were going to turn up some crimes. We patrolled very actively, and by keeping our eyes peeled we managed to catch people involved in three separate cases of housebreaking. She was thrilled to be doing some real police work and her excitement rubbed off on me. The young cops on the shift back at the station had only managed to give out parking tickets and were very envious of Karen's successes.

I showed her how to write up a case properly and how to fingerprint the prisoners. The night just flew. By the end of the shift her eyes were shining.

'You're capable of doing this job,' I said. 'Don't let anyone tell you that you're stupid. Now that you've done it once you'll know how to do it next time. The people on this shift talk the talk but they don't know everything.'

'Thanks,' she beamed. 'I'm really grateful to you.'

She gained more confidence after that, but still found the attitude of the other officers hard to handle.

It wasn't long before the chance came for some sweet revenge against one of the loud young men. His name was Andrew and his ambition was to be a traffic cop. It gave him great pleasure to issue tickets to any motorist who had stepped out of line. One day I was paired up with him and we had to go and collect a warrant from the divisional headquarters in the city centre. I was driving the panda car and had stopped at a red light at a large junction. There was a car on the opposite side of the junction waiting to turn right.

'He's just gone through a red light,' said Andrew indignantly.

'What are you talking about?' I asked. 'You can't see whether the lights are red or not from where we are.'

'Stop the car, stop the car. I'm telling you he went through a red light,' shouted Andrew.

'No, I'm not stopping,' I said. 'Have you got X-ray eyes and can you see round corners? You can't tell if he went through a red light or not.'

I drove off when the lights turned green and stopped at the next set of red lights. The car Andrew insisted had gone through a red light pulled up behind us.

'I'm going to speak to him,' Andrew blurted out. 'He's getting done.'

He jumped out of the passenger seat and banged on the window of the car behind. The lights changed to green and I accelerated sharply, leaving Andrew in the middle of the road. He wasn't able to do anything on his own as Scottish law requires two police to be present before any action can be taken against someone. He was left standing speechless in the middle of the road and had to walk back to the police station.

He arrived back fuming. 'What did you do that for?'

'It was just a load of rubbish about that guy going through a red light. You were on a power trip. Don't ever do that again when you're working with me.'

He hung his head like a naughty schoolboy.

I continued to get along well with Karen and we started to socialize, going out for a meal and a few drinks, not in the style of drunken police nights out but pleasant, grown-up evenings.

One time we went on to a nightclub afterwards and there were some police officers there who Karen knew but I didn't.

She introduced me to Ali, a police officer of Yemeni origin, who I felt instantly attracted to. He was six foot tall, extremely good-looking and very gregarious. One of the things that I liked about him straight away was that he didn't seem like a typical police officer.

We began dancing to Stevie Wonder's 'Superstition'.

'He's one of my favourite singers,' I said, shouting to make myself heard above the music.

'I know. He's great,' said Ali.

'You're some dancer,' I grinned.

'You too.' He grabbed me round the waist, spun me round and kissed me. Normally I would have pushed a guy away if he'd done that so soon after we'd met, but with Ali it just felt right and I kissed him back.

We didn't talk much after that. We found ourselves a quiet corner in the nightclub where we could carry on kissing and gazing into each other's eyes. It felt as if we were the only two people there.

From that night onwards we became inseparable. When we weren't working we spent all our spare time together. He loved rugby, and whereas before he used to watch games at the pub with his pals, now he would do that with me. Most of the time we socialized by ourselves, away from the rest, and we never seemed to run out of things to talk about. We both loved trips to the cinema and going out for meals and we spent more or less every night together at either his flat or mine.

After we'd been seeing each other for a few weeks I arranged to meet Ali in a coffee shop with my mum and sister Kim. Both of them wanted to check him out because I'd been talking about him so much.

When the three of us arrived he was sitting there with a big smile on his face, trying to hide his nervousness. He'd just finished his shift and was still wearing his police shirt and trousers with his own jacket on. I was excited to see him again, and whatever my mum's and sister's verdict was I knew that Ali had already become very special to me. He had three flowers and gave one to each of us. That went down well with the mother-and-sister jury, and we chatted easily for a while.

Then he said to my mum, 'I'm gonna marry your daughter.'

I laughed it off, but hearing that made me feel warm inside. I'd never felt such intense feelings so quickly for anyone before.

My mum started laughing. 'Oh, Anne's a real free spirit you know.'

'We can be free spirits together then,' he said.

He'd passed the test that day, and it wasn't long before he became part of the family.

The next day I was sitting in the report-writing room at the police station when Susan, the young officer who had started at the same time as Michelle, walked in. I asked her how she getting on.

'Fine,' she said. 'Mike's away at the dentist so I'm catching up on some report writing.'

'Are you learning much from him?'

She sighed, and then with her head in her hands began to tell me what it was like to work with Mike.

'He started off by telling me that his wife doesn't understand him, then he says that he really enjoys my company and that he can really be himself with me. Now he always tries to arrange it so that he does the night shift with me, then he keeps on telling me how gorgeous he thinks I am. And he never stops pestering me on my days off, asking me to meet up with him.'

# Sixteen

I hugged Ali as he lifted my case out of the car. I was back at Tulliallan. It was eight years since I'd first walked up the sweeping driveway as a trainee. The place had been spruced up a bit, with some new playing fields and modern buildings that reminded me of Butlins holiday camp accommodation. I saw some of the new recruits panting away as they sprinted round the playing fields.

'Thank God I'm not starting out now,' I said to Ali.

'Me too. I'm gonna miss you, darling.'

'I know. I wish I didn't have to be away from you. But don't worry, I'll be back at the weekend and we can spend lots of time together.'

I didn't get much notice about leaving Kingston Road and going to Tulliallan on a six-week trainee detective course, so I hadn't had a chance to speak to the sergeant about Mike, the predatory cop, before I left. It played on my mind when I found out that he was not only making Michelle's life a misery but Susan's too, and I wondered how many other young female officers were being harassed by Mike and others like him.

Before I left I'd advised both women to speak to each other and to approach the sergeant together.

I was wearing a smart suit for my visit to Tulliallan this time instead of the stiff uniform I'd arrived in first time round. The detective training course had a reputation for being an exercise in drinking solidly for six weeks and for nightly parties in people's rooms.

I had been interviewed by personnel before I was appointed a detective constable, and one of the questions I was asked by the chief inspector there was, 'Do you want to do this job because you see it as a glamorous one?'

'Are you kidding?' I replied. 'What's glamorous about dealing with serious crime? I want to do it because I'm more interested in solving serious crimes than minor ones, and I want to work on bigger cases, to get involved in interviewing suspects and to develop my knowledge.'

That must have been the right thing to say, because I got the job. By now I knew I had to use the police jargon that they loved to hear. I also knew that if you said the wrong thing at CID interviews you could forget about getting a job there.

This time there was no agonizing walk across the parade square. Trainee detectives could slip in through the back door. I picked up the key to my quarters – in contrast with the sparse dormitory I'd slept in last time, I now had a comfortable room with an en suite bathroom. I bumped into a couple of the new recruits in the corridor. They didn't know who I was, but they took one look at my smart suit and called me 'Ma'am'. That made me smile, but it also made me feel quite old. Some of the detectives I'd come across as a new recruit at Tulliallan had been too superior to speak to us newcomers, but I made a point of trying to chat and be friendly, remembering exactly how it felt to be new and not to have a clue what you're supposed to be doing.

There were just five women on my CID course and twenty men. I was the only woman from my division to attend. The requirement to be fit had been ignored, and many of the officers selected were overweight and drank heavily. We had to learn a lot of case law and were expected to write three essays, but there was plenty of scope to manage our own schedules. One of my essays was exploring the maxim of the criminologist Edmond Locard: 'Every contact leaves a trace.' I found the essays quite hard to write because I'd been away from school for so long. We were under pressure to write a specified number of words to tight deadlines, and the work we produced had to be thoroughly researched. Although it was tough, I found that forcing myself to write an essay was a good discipline. The workload for detectives is far heavier than for uniformed officers, and this was a way of preparing us for the kind of pressure we'd be under in our new jobs.

We learnt how to bag up evidence using different bags and different kinds of tape to ensure that evidence in serious cases such as rapes and murders was preserved properly. Some bags were made out of a special kind of plastic to preserve the contents from fires. Even air after a fire can be tested to help find out what caused it – you can go into a building that has been set on fire, take some of the air and simply seal it into a bag.

As new recruits we hadn't been allowed out in the evenings, but this time our evenings were our own and many officers on the detectives' course headed down to the local pub called Garvie's, a crowded, smoky bar largely populated by women, some of whom had been hit with the ugly stick. They waited for each new intake of detectives on the Tulliallan course to find their way down to the pub. Thursday nights were especially popular as there were karaoke sessions. The local women knew the police went home for the weekend the following day and that they would be having a good night out beforehand, so Thursdays were by far the best pick-up nights.

Detectives' courses had a reputation for being drinking marathons, and many officers began their days seriously hung-over, often dragging themselves up the driveway after spending the night with a woman from the village. Sometimes they nodded off during the lectures.

I was drinking too, but for different reasons. Faced with the macho culture of the course and the puffed-up egos of the male detective trainees, I found myself more often than not needing a few glasses of wine to get through the evening. I also sensed that, as with my first visit eight years ago, senior officers were watching us. We were expected to behave in a certain way – and that included socializing. Although I did dutifully go to the bar every evening, and sometimes to the local pub, I knew I wasn't drinking as much as the other trainees and my behaviour was not as rowdy. I also knew this nonconformist behaviour had been noted.

Unlike most of the married detectives on the course, who seemed delighted to be liberated from their wives, I was missing Ali dreadfully and wasn't happy about being away from home. Every evening I called him when my lectures had finished just to hear his voice. He told me funny stories about his day at work to cheer me up, and said that he'd recorded my favourite programmes and that he couldn't wait to see me.

'I really miss you,' I said.

'I miss you too. I can't wait to see you. Don't worry, only three more weeks to go and then you're finished,' he said. 'You know, Anne, I really love you and I want to spend the rest of my life with you. I'm really proud of you for doing the detective course.'

'I love you too,' I said. It was the first time we'd said it to each other and I couldn't stop smiling.

'I've been thinking. We spend every spare moment together and it seems a waste of money to have two flats when we're always in one. Why don't we buy a house together, a nice family house?'

'Don't you think it's a bit too soon? We've only been together for three months.'

'I know how I feel. Don't you?'

'Of course I do, you know that. Maybe you're right. Having two mortgages does seem like a waste of money. We'll start looking when I get home.'

'I've already started,' he said.

'You're crazy! But that's why I love you,' I laughed.

One Thursday evening while I was sitting in the pub cradling a glass of wine I overheard the crudest chat-up line I'd ever come across, when a local woman who had been through squads of detectives in her time sidled up to one of the male detectives and said, 'I take it up the dunny.' I nearly choked on my drink. I'd never heard a woman offering anal sex as an opening gambit before.

I could see one of the inspectors sitting in the corner in a clinch with a woman who obviously wasn't his wife. His hands were cupping her buttocks, pulling her towards him. His wedding ring was clearly visible. A few detectives had commented that he stood at the window watching them stumble up the driveway each morning around 7 am after spending the night with a woman they'd met at Garvie's. They found it unnerving to be watched as they staggered back from their trysts, and couldn't understand what he was up to.

I could hear two guys from my course talking about the woman who was belting out 'D.I.V.O.R.C.E.' accompanied by the karaoke machine. She was about five foot tall, in her fifties, very overweight, with flicked-out, Eighties-style hair, heavy blue eye shadow and an extremely low-cut top that revealed part of her heavy breasts swaying in time to the music.

'I shagged her last week,' the first one said. 'She makes a mean fry-up.'

'I might try my luck tonight, what d'you think?' said the second one.

'Go for it mate, I think you'll be in there. She's giving you the eye.'

Most of the officers were starting to pair up and disappear. I made my way back to my room at Tulliallan feeling very alone and different from the others.

During the day we were presented with various crime scenarios and a few clues and had to do our best to solve them. We were also trained in interviewing suspects on tape. To do this we were paired up and had to critique each other's performances.

Part of the course involved us developing skills in making press statements on TV. Sometimes we did that to appeal for witnesses or information. However, if someone had been arrested we had to be sure not to give out information that could jeopardize his or her chances of getting a fair trial. We were warned that the press might ask leading questions to try and get vital information out of us and we were taught to be very wary. You can see the results of the training when you watch police officers choosing their words very carefully when interviewed on TV.

A TV interviewer was paid to come to the college for the day. He interviewed us all about an invented scenario and then critiqued our performances afterwards. He tried his best to put us under pressure with his persistent questioning. I was quite guarded and he told me I looked nervous. The whole experience made me apprehensive about doing that kind of interview in the future. While it was important that we should make good use of journalists, I wasn't sure that it was helpful to teach us to be so suspicious of them.

We were also taught how to prepare and deliver briefings. We had to make a decision about which cars and officers to deploy where, how to organize staff so as to make the most of their talents, and who would be paired up with who. The key requirement was to make sure that everybody understood their role. I'd experienced this on a smaller scale when I was a Plainer – we were expected to organize ourselves so that everybody was clear about the aims of the next operation. I always looked forward to the challenge of coordinating the team and seeing everyone work together.

Pathologists and forensic scientists came in to give lectures that I found fascinating. They had the ability to make dead people come alive again by giving us vital clues about the final moments of their lives. Every case was different and had a signature of its own. These experts could offer us tools to help crack some of the most difficult and complex crimes. After eight years in the police I knew that these were the kinds of cases I wanted to work on, and I sat in lectures like a sponge, soaking up every word that was said to us.

There was one pathologist in particular who I was very impressed by. She showed us slides of a trip she'd taken to Bosnia and talked us through them. There were open trenches full of bodies, with families huddled around at the top looking for answers about how their loved ones had died. She told us how fulfilling she found it to excavate bones from these mass graves, trying to piece together evidence and offer some answers about what had happened to people's loved ones and how long they had been dead. I could see from the photos how distraught the relatives were, but also how grateful they felt, and how they hugged her because she had given them some closure.

We were also given photos of crime scenes and asked to work out what had happened. There was one photo that showed a bathroom with the walls and ceiling completely splattered with blood. A man and his wife lived in the house and the blood belonged to the wife.

'It must be her husband. Jail him,' said one of the other officers after taking a quick look at the picture. It turned out that although the picture looked like a crime scene straight out of a Hammer House of Horror movie, in fact no offence had been committed. The woman had been shaving her legs in the bath and had cut herself, puncturing a major artery in her leg. Blood had spurted everywhere and she had bled to death.

'The reason for showing you all this picture,' said the

police trainer, 'is so that you understand the importance of not jumping to conclusions when you arrive at the scene of a suspected serious crime. Leave your prejudices and preconceptions outside the door and consider every suspect as an individual, looking at all the available evidence before drawing your conclusions.'

If only.

# Seventeen

As I stood in the ante-room I pulled on my surgical gown, my sterile bath hat, my oversized wellingtons and finally my gloves. I looked as if I was about to perform open-heart surgery, but in fact I was attending a post-mortem and did not have to do anything more technical than label various bagged-up body samples handed to me for analysis by the pathologist. This was one of my new jobs as a CID officer. My colleague Billy and I smiled sheepishly at each other because we knew we looked ridiculous dressed in full scrubs.

After we'd donned our outfits a young, heavily pierced mortuary attendant with a Gothic hairdo and make-up that wouldn't have looked out of place in a Marilyn Manson video signalled to us to go through into the room where the pathologist was working. We pushed the door open and had to walk through a puddle of sterile water like at the swimming baths.

This was my first post-mortem and I was scared. I'd overcome the terror I'd felt as a trainee police officer about seeing dead people, but I'd never before seen the insides of a dead body, nor a living one come to that, and would rather have preserved my ignorance. The place was cold and creepy, with drains in the floors so that the blood could be hosed away. Harsh fluorescent lights shone over the metal table where the naked body lay, and gave the body a yellowish tinge. I knew from other dead bodies I'd seen that the blood of a corpse collects wherever the centre of gravity is. The skin where the blood gathers is a burgundy colour while the skin furthest away from the blood looks waxy and jaundiced.

I had visited the mortuary a year before, but not the post-mortem room, only the back door where bodies were unloaded from the black mortuary hearses. I'd accompanied undertakers bringing in the body of an old woman who had fallen in her bedsit and whose bones were so fragile that she was found lying with her calves unnaturally twisted forwards from the knee, with a bleeding wound to her head. When I arrived at midnight to relieve the late-shift officer who'd been sitting with the body waiting for the mortuary officers to come, the first thing I'd heard in the flat was the sound of a football match coming from the front room. A man's voice shouted, 'Are you fucking blind, referee?'

I walked slowly through the hall, frightened because I hadn't yet seen the body and had been told it was a mangled mess. I pushed open the living-room door and the first thing I saw was the dead woman's legs sticking out, weirdly bent. Then I saw the officer slouching on the sofa, feet up on the coffee table, glued to the Celtic–Rangers highlights on the TV, tie and jacket off. My eyes were drawn to the body but his remained fixed on the TV screen.

'I've come to let you get away,' I said hesitantly.

'Good timing. It's the last minute of the game.' He stood up and put his tie and jacket back on.

'Have you been here long?' I asked.

'Ay. The mortuary attendants are busy. There are a lot of dead bodies tonight. That's why we're having to wait so long.'

He handed me the TV remote control as he was leaving. 'Just watch the telly, hen.'

I didn't want him to leave because it gave me the creeps to be left on my own with the body. I would have given anything for him to plant his oversized bottom back on the sofa, and would even have been prepared to watch the game with him. After he left I sat on the edge of the sofa with my escape route planned, one foot propping the door open. I didn't put the telly on because I had to be sure of hearing every sound. Each time I glanced at the body it seemed to have shifted position. I'd never been so scared of an old woman. The time dragged and I made call after call on the radio, asking for an update about when the mortuary attendants would come.

I sat there for another hour till at last, to my huge relief, two men in black suits walked in. They looked like the two old men in the Muppets who sit in the balcony. They calmly unfolded the body and stowed it unceremoniously in a body bag. I accompanied them to the car and had to sit next to the body in the back while they sat in the front. The back of the car was in darkness, and I was convinced that the old woman's hand was going to shoot out of the body bag and drag itself up my leg.

'What you having for your dinner, Bert?' one of the men asked the other.

'How do you cope with all these dead bodies day after day?' I asked. I could hardly believe that they could be so detached from the gruesome realities of their job.

'At least ours don't fight back, hen,' he said. He obviously thought his job was easier than mine, but I preferred to stick with the living. The two men chattered on about the deaths they'd dealt with that night. One body they'd picked up had been lying in a flat for a while and was crawling with maggots. When we reached the back doors of the mortuary I had to go in with them and watch them strip the body. All the bodies in Glasgow were brought here, and there were more than twenty fridges to store them in.

I was jolted back into the present when I saw a couple of senior detectives come and stand behind the viewing screen in the post-mortem room. The police were particularly interested in this case – a drug-dealer had been found dead in his car, and because it wasn't clear how he'd died it was being treated as a suspicious death. There were rumours that either the police or figures in the underworld had been involved. The police didn't like this man because he had successfully sued them a few years before for attacking him with a baseball bat during a drugs raid at his home. I knew him because he lived near my family and I had given some background information about him and his family to the officers looking into his death.

I was no longer shocked at the sight of a dead body, but couldn't help shuddering at the prospect of seeing it opened up. My fingers kept clenching and unclenching as I prepared for the worst. Trying to ignore the acrid smell of disinfectant, which burned my nostrils, I forced myself to watch as the pathologist examined the body for any cuts, bruises or wounds to the skin. There were a few bruises on his knees and elbows but he decided they weren't suspicious. He picked up his scalpel and began to cut. He slit the body vertically from throat to groin, then pulled apart the skin to expose the organs. I could see a spongy yellow layer between the skin and the bones that was obviously fat. It looked revolting. As soon as the pathologist started cutting I felt that this man I used to know ceased to be a person and was simply a body, with no more connection to life than a dummy. But losing that sense of a person didn't make the dissecting ritual any less grotesque. I was starting to feel queasy but was also strangely fascinated and couldn't look away.

Systematically the pathologist lifted out his heart, liver and the rest of his organs and began to examine them. All of the organs looked like the kind of cuts of meat you'd pick up at the butcher's. He inspected each organ for damage or abnormalities. Anything that looked normal he left intact, only taking samples of the organs that gave him cause for concern.

'Oh, I see he had a beef curry for dinner,' he said when he began to examine the contents of his stomach. I hadn't realized that during a post-mortem it was possible to work out the last thing a person had eaten before they died.

When he moved on to the lungs he said, 'I can see there's a lot of smoking-related damage here.'

Each time he cut a small sample from an organ he bagged it up, then passed it to Billy or me to label. I was relieved that there was a plastic bag separating me from the body bits. Several blood samples were taken and dispatched to a unit at Glasgow University where they would be tested for traces of drugs, alcohol or disease.

After he'd finished with the body the pathologist moved on to the head, cutting the skin and bone from the top of the skull in a pudding-basin shape. Then he lifted off the top of the skull to reveal the brain, a spongy ball of grey matter with lines on it, which he pulled out. After he'd finished I couldn't believe my eyes when he bundled the organs he'd finished examining into a bin bag and stuffed them back inside the body. Then he signalled to two of his assistants to sew the dead man up. It had been a gruesome experience, but I was surprised and relieved that I could look at a body being cut open without being sick.

The body looked peculiarly lumpy afterwards, very different from the way it had looked before it had been cut open.

'That's him all stitched up,' quipped one of the detectives watching the proceedings through the glass screen. The other one roared with laughter.

The post-mortem room was similar to a wet room and the assistants hosed away the bits of blood and guts that had leaked onto the floor.

It was a huge relief when it was over. My stomach was still jittery, but I knew that after what I'd just seen I'd never again be scared of even the most gruesome horror movie.

A police photographer was there, and once he'd taken all the official shots he needed he took a photo of Billy and me in our scrubs for a souvenir.

Once the body had been tidied up I was asked to fingerprint him, something not usually done to a dead body, but we wanted to check if his prints had been found at any other crime scenes. His fingers were stiffly bent and it wasn't easy, but I did my best and managed to get a print.

Billy and I drove back to the police station together. It was his first post-mortem too and he looked pale and shaken. I felt no better, and we said little as we walked. We each knew exactly how the other one was feeling.

The CID office was open-plan and I could hear Detective Constable Logan laughing and joking on the phone. I had taken a particular dislike to him. He was a vain and smarmy man who considered himself to have a way with the ladies. He lolled back in his swivel chair and flicked ash into a nearby ashtray as he chatted.

'Well, you know what they say mate, policewomen are only good for two things – fucking and frying.'

I was more repelled by him than ever when I heard that misogynistic bile spew out of his mouth. He finished his phone conversation then swivelled his chair round to face me, giving me his usual 'undressing' look.

'So how was your first post-mortem, hen?' he asked. Without waiting for a reply he continued, 'Just in time to put the kettle on for us boys.'

'Do it yourself,' I retorted. 'You should be making me tea because I've just got back in from the post-mortem.'

He grunted and I walked into the kitchen area and made myself a cup of coffee but didn't offer DC Logan one. I heard Billy asking Logan what he was working on.

'That old woman who got raped. The bastard stole her purse. At least we've got CCTV footage of him following her to the flats.'

One of the phones rang and Billy picked it up. 'No problem, I'll let her know,' I heard him say. He put the phone down and turned to me.

'That was the uniform bar. Paul Walker is locked up. He's asking for you.'

I went to my desk, got out the pack of cigarettes in the drawer and picked up a newspaper that was a couple of days old. I'd arrested Paul Walker for car theft a few times before and knew he'd be grateful for both.

'That wee scumbag car thief only wants to gie you a turn cos he's locked up for the weekend and wants out,' said DC Logan.

I turned around and said irritably, 'What's it got to do with you?' I loathed him so much I felt contaminated just by being in the same room with him and having to breathe the same air.

I walked through to the cells and got the male turnkey to get Paul Walker out and escort him to one of the interview rooms. Paul was about eighteen years old, lanky with teenage spots, and was wearing a tracksuit. He sat down and flashed me a smile of recognition.

'How are you doing, Paul?' I asked, handing him a cigarette.

'No bad. That cell's doing my head in though.'

'How did you get locked up this time?' I asked.

'I tanned an Aston Martin, fucking belter, Ah've no stole one of them before, but it wis too much of a stick-out and they traffic cops fae Brown Street caught me. If ah'd been on the motorway ah'd have left them standing wi' their shite BMW.'

Car thieves are the only criminals who like to boast about their exploits. Often when they are charged with one theft they will happily confess to several others. They want to relive the thrill of taking the car and racing it, and talking to a police officer (or anyone else who'd listen) allows them to do that. They are always looking for a faster, better car to drive. Teenagers like Paul wouldn't look twice at a clapped-out, second-hand car. Half the thrill for them is getting behind the wheel of something top-of-the-range that they've never driven before. Working out how to circumvent the security system is part of the fun. I had locked up Paul several times and knew him quite well.

'How's your ma?' I asked, using his language to make him feel comfortable.

'Fed up wi' me getting locked up. She wants me to get a job,' he said, taking another drag on his cigarette.

'Maybe you should listen. I'm sure she's sick of having the police at the door.'

'She's sick of they drug-dealing bastards up the stairs as well. She's worried about ma wee brother finding dirty needles.'

'I thought that family had stopped after getting turned last week?'

'Naw. It's started again. There's a lot of activity at lunchtime every day. Ah think their gear gets delivered in the morning cos the place is crawling with junkies about one o'clock looking to score.'

'You could make some money for providing this kind of information to us, Paul.'

'I don't give a fuck aboot the money. I hate those scum bastards and worry about ma wee brother.'

I laughed. 'Maybe getting paid could stop you stealing cars. You could become a racing driver, or better still a traffic polis.'

He laughed. 'I'm too fast for them. Besides, I drive better motors.'

He finished his cigarette. I gave him the newspaper to read

and asked the turnkey to take him back to his cell. Then I headed back to the CID office to write up an intelligence report about the information Paul had just given me.

As I walked back into the office I heard Billy say to DC Logan, 'Have you seen the CCTV footage of the Stilley murder?'

'Ay, it's shocking isn't it?' said DC Logan. Then Billy turned to me and asked me if I'd seen it. I shook my head.

'Go and watch it. It's through there in the video room.'

I walked into the video room and put the clearly labelled video on. I didn't know much about it other than that it was a murder that had been caught on CCTV. With most murders we only saw the aftermath and I was very apprehensive about seeing something horrific unfold on film.

The video was shot in Argyll Street, one of the busiest in Glasgow. It was mid-evening, about the time when the population in the area triples as lots of people come into the centre to go to bars and nightclubs. Two young boys appeared on the video footage. Both were wearing baseball caps and one was showing the other something that appeared to be a knife. He was waving it around boastfully and it looked to me as if he was itching to use it. A middle-aged man came into view and the boy with the knife nudged his friend as if to say, 'He's getting it.'

He walked up to the man and bumped into him. The man stepped back and held his hands out in a defensive gesture. The other boy intervened and indicated to his friend something like, 'No, not him,' as if he knew him. The man walked off, probably not realizing quite how lucky an escape he'd had. A few minutes later two middle-aged couples appeared on the camera. Once again the boy with the knife indicated that one of them was 'getting it'. He shouted something, which I discovered later was, 'Your wife's a cow.'

One of the middle-aged men shouted something back which I later learned was, 'Away you go son.'

The boy with the knife made his way towards him and stabbed him repeatedly in the chest. The man stumbled out onto the road, fell down and died instantly.

I felt sick as I watched it. The CCTV operator had seen it unfold and kept the camera on the two boys as they ran off. The stabber was seen discarding the knife on the corner of Buchanan Street. Because the CCTV operator had done such a good job the police were on the scene very quickly and caught the boys. They had just turned sixteen, and the one who murdered the man was sent to jail for life. Later, during another enquiry, I interviewed a teacher who had taught this boy. She told me that he came from a background where he didn't stand a chance, his family being involved in drugs and violence. Apparently he'd been watching a violent video just before he went out with his knife.

I left the video room in shock. Premeditated murders are rare and it's even rarer for them to be captured on CCTV. I wondered how that poor man's wife must have felt, happily walking along the street with her husband one minute and watching him die the next. Sometimes I found it hard to get my head round how cruel life could be. There was no justice in who was struck down before their time. Life was fragile and survival a lottery.

I wandered down to the control room to speak to the uniformed staff and see if there were any prisoners I needed to interview. The duty sergeant handed me a telex which had been circulated to other police forces from a force down south. It was usual practice to send on information about crimes with an unusual modus operandi. I took the telex back up to the CID room, and as I read it a shiver ran down my spine.

A woman was driving home alone along a dual carriage-way when she saw a baby wrapped up and lying by the roadside. She was shocked and pulled over to have a look. When she got close to it she discovered that it was just a doll swaddled in blankets. Feeling scared, she ran back to her car and drove off as fast as she could. In her rear-view mirror she could see a man in the car behind her flashing his headlights all the time. This went on for about two miles with the car staying close on her tail. She searched desperately for some-where safe to stop to get away from him, and eventually found a hotel in a village and pulled up in front of it. The man flash-ing his headlights screeched to a halt behind her. She rushed out of her car and banged on the door of the hotel. Her pur-suer ran up to her and grabbed her by the shoulder.

'There's someone in your car,' he said. 'He jumped into the back when you stopped the car and walked to the grass verge. I've been flashing you to warn you ever since.'

The police were called and it turned out that there was indeed a man in the car, and he was holding a knife. She hadn't noticed him because he had lain down very still on the back seat. The man turned out to be a convicted rapist and the sharp-eyed motorist may well have saved her life. If he hadn't seen the rapist get into the car and if the woman had been killed, nobody would have known how he had done it. I wanted to know whether the rapist had stayed hidden in the car until the police arrived or whether he'd tried to make a run for it. But this wasn't explained in the bulletin because it is only the briefest details about the crime that are circulated, the aim being to alert police officers to unusual criminal methods.

I was desperate to get out of the police station and home to Ali. I'd encountered more than enough horror and misery for one day. We'd bought a house together five months before and things were going fantastically well between us. I fell into his arms when he opened the door.

'I've had a terrible day,' I said. 'I'm so glad to be home.'

Ali had cooked me a delicious meal and he ran me a bath and lit candles around it to relax me. Being with him helped to take away the pain of the day. He had been in the police for just a few years and worked on a uniformed shift in Paisley, a rough working-class town outside Glasgow. He loved what he did and was ambitious to get on in the job. I told him about all the horrible things that had happened during my shift and he listened sympathetically. As I lay in the bath I tried to forget about it all, but every time I closed my eyes images of the man I'd seen fatally stabbed on CCTV bled into those of the body lying in the mortuary and the unsuspecting woman who drove her car with a rapist curled up on the back seat.

# Eighteen

I pushed open the door of the briefing room and saw a sea of male suits. As I squeezed past the officers already seated to reach one of the few remaining vacant chairs, one of them leered at me and hissed under his breath, 'Your arse looks great in that suit.'

I gave him a dirty look and made my usual response: 'Fuck off!'

Like most of the female officers I got comments like that all the time, and although I tried my best not to let them get to me I found them increasingly distressing.

I was becoming more and more disenchanted with the behaviour of some of my male colleagues. They all looked so respectable in their suits and ties, but along with the leering remarks came the drunken behaviour. Many police officers drank heavily but CID officers had a particular reputation for knocking back copious amounts of alcohol. Earlier that morning a dishevelled officer who had got very drunk the night before had driven himself into work, breathalysed himself in the office and found he was still over the limit. He started pouring black coffee down his throat in the hope that he'd sober up before any of the bosses noticed his condition.

The breathalysing trick was a popular one, and officers who were feeling rough after a heavy night sometimes bedded down in an empty police cell in the hope of sleeping off their hangover. Miraculously, officers generally got away with coming into work still drunk from the night before. Either colleagues covered up for them, or years of experience had taught them how to cover their tracks. A lot of the hardened drinkers didn't seem to get drunk despite downing vast amounts of alcohol.

Apart from having to put up with the sexist drunkards, I loved being in the CID. I'd been in the department for about a year now and had my own desk, my own cases and various regular work partners. I found it stimulating dealing with more serious, complex crimes and had more time to pursue criminals than when I was in uniform. The workload was heavier than in the uniformed police so it was important to prioritize and to use initiative. I really liked being able to see a lengthy inquiry through from beginning to end rather than just being involved in a small part of it – it gave me a better overview of the criminal justice system. The work was deadline-oriented, and we were constantly up against it to submit complex crime reports to the procurator fiscal within strict time limits.

The briefing was about the arrest of a Sikh woman, Gurmit Bassi, in connection with the murder of another Sikh woman, Rani Bassi. At first the victim's husband, Harbej Bassi, had been the chief suspect, but he'd been working in his restaurant at the time of the murder and so was ruled out early on. A witness had seen Gurmit and a man at the scene and had watched them leave in a taxi. It had been traced and the driver had confirmed that he'd taken a couple to Cambuslang, on the outskirts of Glasgow, where Gurmit lived.

The superintendent handed out various jobs to people. The guys were given all the cushy tasks but my name was much further down the list. Everyone wanted to interview the suspect, but there was no chance of me being asked to do that. It was a case of jobs for the boys.

I was sent to Cambuslang to try and trace the man Gurmit had been seen with. She had named him as Christopher Jones, and I found out that he worked in her local grocery store. I took a statement from him and he claimed that he had been with Gurmit in the Woodlands area of Glasgow where the murder had been committed, but had waited in the taxi and didn't know anything about a killing. There wasn't enough evidence to arrest him.

I returned to the office and was told to go and find PC Singh, the only Sikh officer in the force, and to go to the local temple with him to find Sikh women who would be prepared to act as stand-ins – take part in an identity parade.

Usually it wasn't a problem getting stand-ins: people were paid £10 for doing the job and we put notices up in the local homeless hostels. It was the only time that criminals were clamouring to get into police cars, because people who were in desperate need of money to support a drug habit could earn a reasonable amount if they participated in a lot of identity parades. It would be much harder finding Sikh women in their thirties to get involved, however.

I found PC Singh in the report-writing room. He was a

pleasant, good-looking young officer who wore a turban. We headed off to the temple in the Woodlands area, where there was a large Asian community and where the murder had taken place. On the way we chatted. PC Singh told me he had just come back from another photo shoot with the chief constable and spoke glumly about the way he was pulled out of police work frequently to pose for pictures to prove what an enlightened, politically correct and ethnically diverse police force Glasgow had. 'Thank God I'm getting an opportunity to do some real police work for a change,' he said. 'I didn't join the force just to get my photo taken.'

I thought about how bad that must make him feel, knowing that his policing skills were less important than the colour of his skin as far as senior officers were concerned. Ali – like every non-white officer in Strathclyde – had been used for this purpose and I knew he loathed it too.

We went into the temple and took off our shoes. PC Singh did all the talking, explaining in Punjabi why we were there. The people in the temple were appalled by the murder and wanted to do everything they could to help. They made us feel very welcome and gave us a meal of rice and dhal. After we'd explained what we wanted, six of the women agreed to take part in the identity parade, which took place a few days later. The suspect was picked out and one of the officers hissed, 'She's an evil black bitch.' When the public saw the smiling posters of black or Asian police officers apparently having the time of their lives in the job they would never suspect just how endemic racist remarks like these were in the force.

I knew that the white male police officers who dominated the force put all of us in boxes. The woman who was suspected of the murder was in one box, I was in another because I was a woman and a suspected Catholic, and Ali was in another because he wasn't white.

After Gurmit Bassi had been picked out in the identity parade she was charged with murder. By this time enough evidence had been gathered against Christopher Jones, a former butcher, to charge him with murder as well.

When the case came to court a horrific story unfolded. Police had discovered Rani Bassi dead on the floor of the flat she shared with her husband Harbej in Woodlands Drive, Glasgow, on 13 April 1998. It was the date of Basaki, the Sikh spring festival. The walls and floor were sprayed with blood and Rani had been stabbed and slashed. A cross had been carved into her back and her head was almost severed. She had been pregnant and a knife had slashed open her womb in an attempt to cut out her unborn baby.

Rani had moved to Scotland from the Punjab a year before and had married Harbej. But Harbej's first wife Gurmit was still on the scene. The couple had two children together, but Gurmit began to have mental health problems and spent time in a psychiatric hospital. She claimed that her husband was a mass murderer and that their home was full of snakes and small animals that lived inside her. Her mental health problems led to the break-up of their marriage, although the couple continued to have sex, even after Harbej married Rani. Their two sons moved in with Harbej and Rani. Harbej decided to end the relationship with Gurmit when Rani became pregnant, a development that wasn't well received by Gurmit.

On the night of the murder Gurmit called her fourteen-year-old son Steven and asked him to come into the street and bring the house keys with him. He did this and found his mother standing outside with a man he didn't know – Christopher Jones.

Gurmit told Steven to wait outside while she and Christopher went upstairs to the flat. When he asked her why, she said that she had paid a man £1,000 to kill Rani's unborn baby and that Harbej really loved her, Gurmit, and wanted this to happen.

Jones initially denied any involvement in the brutal killing, but his partner, Anne McBarron, gave evidence against him, saying that he returned home that night with blood on his hands. That was the evidence police needed to charge him.

The case went to Glasgow's High Court in December 1998. Both Gurmit and Christopher pleaded not guilty and claimed that the other one had carried out the killing. A neighbour said he had heard Rani cry, 'Leave me alone, you dog.'

'Dog' is a term which in Punjabi is only ever applied to males. The jury convicted both of them of murdering Rani and sentenced them to life.

I was relieved that both these brutal killers had been brought to justice and was pleased that good detective work had helped get the case to court. But the murder left me feeling low. I thought a lot about Rani, a young woman I'd never met, what her hopes and dreams might have been when she first arrived in Glasgow and the terrifying way her life ended. However hard I tried I couldn't shake the haunting scene of crime photos of her butchered body out of my mind. She had obviously tried to run away from the frenzied attack as her back was covered in slash marks.

I had joined the CID because I wanted to help solve serious crimes, but I didn't realize how much they would affect me. The more murders, rapes and brutal attacks I worked on the more I was bombarded with the cruellest, darkest side of human nature. Many officers dealt with this by becoming emotionally hardened, or by drinking heavily in an attempt to forget the filth they had to wade through every day. I knew I too was beginning to rely heavily on alcohol as a way to escape the scenes of horror I was witnessing, but I was determined not to join so many other officers on that slippery slope. I didn't want to become that kind of person.

# Nineteen

The club was jumping and the multi-coloured strobes were flashing. On the dance floor the girls wearing white bras were regretting it as their underwear glowed in the lighting. There was lots of talent and a DJ was playing Culture Club.

I was eighteen and was having a night out with my cousin. We usually went to the students' union, but that night we decided to splash out and go to a proper nightclub. She paid my entrance fee because she was getting a student bursary at the college and I'd just left school.

A good-looking guy came up to me and smiled. 'Are you dancing?' he asked. He spoke with an English accent.

'Can ye not think of a better line than that?' I grinned.

He looked crestfallen. I grabbed his hand and said, 'I'm only joking.'

We moved onto the dance floor. It was packed with sweaty, heaving bodies. The men were doused with cheap aftershave and wore *Miami Vice* shirts while the women had big hair and wore ra-ra skirts and fingerless gloves. Flashing boxes underneath the floor turned it different colours.

The guy introduced himself as Jonathan, shouting over Boy George belting out 'Do you really want to hurt me?'

When the song had finished he bought me a cider and blackcurrant and we went and sat in a quiet corner where we could hear ourselves talk.

'What do you do?' I asked him.

'I'm a policeman in London.'

'God, that must be really interesting. I fancy the police force myself. You must see some things.'

'Yes, you sometimes see the worst side of life,' he said. 'And how about you?'

'I've just started working in a big hotel here. I'm dying to get my first pay cheque. I don't think it's as interesting as your job. What's the worst thing you've ever had to deal with?'

'I'm a uniformed bobby so I don't get that much serious crime, but I once had to deal with a rape.'

'That's terrible. What happened?'

'I was out on the beat myself and all of a sudden I heard crying from one of the lanes. I raced over there to see what was going on. There was a girl there, lying semi-naked. She looked scared shitless and was curled up in a ball. I tried to get nearer to her but she just curled up tighter. She was shielding her face from me. I was really shocked and didn't know what to do. It turned out some bastard had raped her. The last thing she needed at that moment was to have another man standing over her, even though I wanted to help. I told her that I could take her down to the police station and she'd be looked after but she refused to come with me.'

'Why didn't she want to complain to the police?'

'You'd be surprised, a lot of women don't report rape.'

'What do you mean? If I was raped I'd go straight to the police.'

'Are you sure about that? It's harder than you think to just walk into a police station and say, "I've been raped." A lot of women are ashamed about this kind of attack and blame themselves.'

I was taken aback. I'd always assumed that I'd immediately report a rape, but now he'd made me think about the realities of actually doing so. At the end of the evening we didn't exchange phone numbers. There seemed little point when we lived so far apart. I said goodbye to him when my cousin and I left the club and never saw him again.

Not long after I joined the CID uniformed officers found a naked and battered young woman crawling along the high street near to the police office. They covered her up and brought her in. DS Donny McGregor took charge. He was a nice man and a good detective and he dealt with the case sensitively and diligently.

It turned out that the young woman had been drinking with friends earlier in the evening in a local bar. A man she didn't know got chatting to one of her friends, joined them at their table and stayed with them until closing time, by which time she'd had quite a few drinks, liked the guy and felt comfortable with him. When the pub closed she agreed to go back to his flat, which was near the pub and a stone's throw away from the police office.

He chatted and joked with her all the way home. But as soon as he closed the door of his flat behind them everything changed. He pushed her from behind and quickly bolted the door. Then he came at her like a wild beast and tore her clothes off before violently raping her.

He started beating and punching her all over, then he turned her over, tied her up and sodomized her. This went on for several hours. He continually raped and sodomized her until he fell asleep and she managed to escape. In a complete daze she wandered out into the street naked. That's where the police officers found her.

They discovered horrendous bruises all over her body that were consistent with her story, and the rape exam found DNA from the man. He was arrested very quickly as she was able to identify where he lived.

DS McGregor asked me to run the ID parade for the case. The officer doing this has to be someone who isn't involved with other aspects of the incident. On the day of the parade the accused man tried to alter his appearance by cutting his hair very short, but the victim and her friends were able to pick him out. I spoke to her afterwards. She was shaking uncontrollably and was visibly in shock at seeing her attacker again, but what struck me most was the sheer anger she felt towards him – she was a nice, sweet girl who put her trust in him and he'd taken advantage of that trust in the worst way imaginable. I was glad to see that she had a lot of close friends and family supporting her after the ordeal she'd endured. There was no doubt she'd need them for quite some time.

I heard DS McGregor say to her, after she'd picked him out, 'You did really well, you're very brave.'

She thanked him and seemed grateful for the way he was handling the case. She trusted him and they had obviously struck up a rapport.

I walked through to pay the stand-ins used in the parade. There have to be a minimum of five and a maximum of eight for any one accused person, all of similar general appearance. Usually in identity parades the witnesses are very frightened because they're worried about getting seen by the accused. Whenever I ran a parade I took all the witnesses into the parade room, put them behind the glass and took half to the other side to reassure them that they couldn't be seen. Even though witnesses know logically that they can't be seen they speak quietly because they're scared.

All the stand-ins are given a number and the witnesses call out the number. Then the person on the parade with that number steps forward to allow the witness a closer look. The accused's lawyer is always present to ensure that things are done fairly and the two police officers running the parade aren't allowed to leave the room once things have started. An officer sits with the witnesses and another one is stationed outside the room to meet them on their way out. The witnesses are referred to by number rather than name. The officer asks them who they have picked out and takes a statement from them. After every witness used, the accused is given the opportunity to move position in the line so that things are completely fair to him or her.

When I walked into the small interview room where the stand-ins waited after the parade to get paid, the first thing that hit me was the overpowering smell of smoke and sweat. They were all smoking roll-ups and a lot of them were homeless. The atmosphere was raucous; they were all in a good mood because they were about to receive the princely sum of £10. I recognized most of them from jailing them on other occasions. As I took the money out of my pocket one of the guys said to me, 'I hope that prick gets life.'

'Ay, he's a fucking beast. Imagine raping women, that's pure scum.'

These men were quite happy to break into houses, but when it came to committing crimes they had their standards and were disgusted by offences like rape and by vicious or sexual attacks on children or old people. Most of the criminals I came across did have some kind of value system, and had boundaries that they wouldn't cross. Only a very small minority seemed downright evil.

I'd heard about one man, who thankfully I'd never met, called Paul Howell. Everybody was frightened of him including his lawyer and the police. He was used as an enforcer by dealers and gangsters, against users who hadn't paid them. His repertoire included sadistically buggering straight men (he was gay), burning them with hot irons and pouring boiling water over them. Most criminals were terrified of him and he was acquitted on quite a few charges because witnesses didn't dare testify against him. He was finally caught when he abducted some teenagers from a care home and forced them to stab and burn each other, keeping them prisoner in his house for several days. A policeman had been sent to the door after calls about a disturbance and ended up not going into the house because he was on his own – a lucky escape for him. The crime came to light when the teenagers escaped and told their social worker what had been going on. They're now in witness protection and their tormentor thankfully was sent to prison. Howell was a man with no morals and no conscience. For him the more he tortured the more pleasure he got.

'Was it no you who jailed me aboot a month ago break-ing into the back of R.S. McColl?' said one of the stand-ins chirpily, breaking into my thoughts.

I looked at him. 'Oh ay, Joseph, I remember now. What happened at court?'

'I got oot on bail for that.'

'You're a pure nightmare man, getting caught,' said Rab, one of the other stand-ins, to him.

'Nae more of that for me. I've met a wee bird now and she's keeping me clean.'

'That's great Joseph, you're looking better. I hope you stick with it. I'm happy to hear that you're retiring from crime.'

'That polis you were wie was a big bastard. He kept tight-ening the cuffs.'

'Ay, was that that DC Finlay? He tried to fit me up with robbery. Is he on the day?' asked Rab.

'I think he's around somewhere,' I said.

'Keep him oot of here,' said Joseph.

As I started handing out the money another stand-in called Tam said, 'You're too good-looking to be polis.' I started laughing and said, 'I bet you say that to all the policewomen.'

He laughed too, revealing two sets of toothless gums.

'Are you chatting her up?' demanded Rab.

'Fuck off, she's alright,' he said.

'Not bad for a bird,' agreed Joseph.

The rape case went to Edinburgh High Court after the accused pleaded not guilty and the girl was forced to give evi-dence. DS McGregor supported her through the trial that lasted for almost a week, and I was there with him, waiting to give evidence about the ID parade.

All the witnesses did well on the stand and the rapist was convicted and received a life sentence.

'I hope you rot in hell, you bastard,' her family shouted. It was a very emotional time. Outside the courthouse the woman was sobbing and hugged DS McGregor. There was some sort of closure for her in seeing the rapist convicted and we were all pleased that justice had been done.

DS McGregor drove me back to Glasgow.

'That poor lassie's been so traumatized,' he said. 'I hope she can start to put it all behind her now. She was in a terrible state after it happened and couldn't eat or sleep. But after he was charged she seemed to get stronger. She was determined to see him convicted so that he couldn't do that to somebody else.'

I could see that DS McGregor was quite emotional himself about the verdict and really felt for the victim. I was glad he'd handled the case so well.

A few months later I was with another officer on night shift CID covering the city centre office. A call came in that a twenty-year-old girl called Paula Brownlow had been dragged into an alleyway behind a nightclub and raped against the wall. The police had taken the woman to the police office and I went to the scene to gather what evidence I could. Whilst I did this the duty officer tried to contact the on-call Female and Child Unit officer who could take a statement from the victim and sit with her in the police rape suite while a doctor examined her and took samples of any evidence the rapist had left on her body.

The alleyway was sealed off when we got there and a uniformed officer was standing at the entrance. It was too dark to see much but as we walked into the alleyway we spotted broken glass and some blood. The alley was full of black rubbish sacks and I shivered thinking about what had just happened in this dank, smelly place. We called out the forensic people and a photographer to gather as much evidence as they could from the scene. I was told that the duty officer hadn't been able to get hold of anyone from Female and Child, so I would have to deal with the victim.

I left the scene and went back to Douglas Road police station in the city centre where the girl had been taken. It didn't have a rape suite, and the nearest one was at Deanspark, which was five miles away, so I called the casualty surgeon, Dr Scott, who would be doing the rape exam, and asked him to meet me there.

Before I walked into the interview room where Paula was waiting I took a deep breath. I felt dread in my stomach trying to imagine what sort of state she'd be in, and thought once again of the dismal alley where she had been raped.

Paula was a small, thin girl who'd had quite a lot to drink and couldn't remember too much about what had happened to her. She was still drunk but recalled enough to sit sobbing with her head in her hands.

'It's gonna be OK, Paula. I'll be with you. The examination won't take too long and it'll help us try to catch the man who did this to you.'

She nodded, wiped her eyes and followed me out to the car.

At Deanspark I took her up to the rape suite, asked her to take her clothes off and gave her a paper gown to wear. The clothes she took off were placed in a bag so they could be used as evidence. An officer went to her home to get fresh clothes for her to change into after the examination.

Rape suites were a relatively recent addition to police stations and weren't yet available everywhere. They consisted of a toilet with a shower, a comfortable sitting room, and a room where the doctor did the examination. It was kitted out with test tubes to put samples into, and syringes, swabs and special bags to preserve the evidence.

Once she'd changed into the gown I asked Paula to sit on the examination bed. Dr Scott introduced himself and was very sympathetic.

'I'm here to help you,' he said, explaining that he needed to take some samples to get evidence of the rape and reassuring her that it wouldn't be painful. She was pale and weepy but she managed to nod her head. She held my hand while the samples were being taken, squeezing it tightly. I could feel her distress and discomfort and winced as I thought about how I would feel if that had happened to me. There were some cuts to her legs and body that the doctor noted.

He took a variety of swabs and some cuttings of pubic hair. Once the examination was over I took Paula into the lounge while the doctor wrote up his findings. She got changed into the fresh clothes and spoke to the doctor. He told me that there was some swelling and bruising around her vagina that could have been caused by someone forcing himself on her. Some samples had been taken which were possibly semen but which needed to be checked at the lab.

I thanked him and preserved the samples. Then I had to interview Paula. A female uniformed constable joined me to do the interview. I tried to get as much detail as I could from her, but it was difficult because she couldn't remember much. It was the first time I'd done a rape exam – it was something

I hadn't been trained for, as it was a job normally done by the Female and Child Unit. If female officers from the unit had been on duty I never would have met Paula. Seeing the young girl in the state she was in made me want to make sure I'd done everything I possibly could to help her case. After I'd done the interview with her I didn't have any further involvement in her case and never found out if the rapist was caught, charged and convicted, although I sometimes thought about her and hoped that she was getting over her ordeal and starting to move on with her life.

I was shocked when I first realized how common rape actually was. To me it was something taboo and very rare, yet it seemed to be almost a weekly occurrence in Glasgow. Rape is such a dreadful thing to happen, and unless you've experienced it I don't think you can possibly understand what the victim is going through. Someone who has been raped feels dirty, humiliated and vulnerable and it takes them years to get over it. I could understand how having to relive the ordeal in court would intensify the trauma.

I thought of Jonathan, the English policeman I'd met so many years ago. Now I understood what he'd meant when he said how difficult it was for a woman to report rape.

# Twenty

We drove at speed down Kilbowie Road in Clydebank then screeched to a halt at the police cordon and jumped out. The whole of the road had been sealed off. It was a busy thoroughfare and the diverted traffic was stuck in jams. I was paired up with DS John Green, who was much more experienced than I was. Adrenalin kicked in and my heart was pounding. I was keen to reach the scene as soon as possible so that I could get to work.

The first thing I saw was the police tent covering a body. Officers in white space-type suits were gathering forensic evidence from it and anything useful around it. Some of the officers had substantial paunches that made them look like Teletubbies in their special outfits.

I could see the ballistics vans parked on the road with the words 'Support Unit' written on the side. The ballistics team was made up of police and civilians. The whole place was swarming with police officers and a police helicopter hovered overhead.

We both jumped out of the car.

'Where will we start?' I asked DS Green. We were going to knock on the doors of all the residents in the street.

'You take 400 to 435 and I'll take 435 to 470 then we'll meet up. Radio me if you get anything.'

I grabbed my clipboard and statement paper out of the back of the car, made my usual check to see if I had a pen and walked off. Pens were still hard to track down, but I was used to it by now and always made sure I had one in my pocket.

The forms used in major inquiries were known as personal descriptive forms. We were expected to record details of vehicles, tattoos, dates of birth and any other relevant information that witnesses had seen or knew about previously. We also had to make sure that we interviewed all the members of a household rather than just the person who happened to be at home when we knocked on the door. I walked up the path of number 400 and tapped on the door of the ground-floor flat. An elderly man appeared.

'Hello, I'm DC Anne Ramsay from Williamstone CID. We're investigating a murder. Do you mind if I come in?'

'Nae bother, come on in, hen. I saw all the police cars. What's going on? I've been at the window all morning.'

'That's great, that's what I'm here to talk to you about,' I said. 'I need to get some details from you.'

He shot back to the window, unable to tear himself away from the action outside. Eventually I managed to get his name and some other basic details from him. 'Did you see anything?' I asked firmly, trying to get his attention.

'Ay, I saw all the police cars arriving and the tent getting put up. It's exciting, isn't it?'

'I need to find out everybody in the area's movements at 8 am this morning.'

'Och, I was in my bed at that time. All the commotion woke me up and I've been trying to find out what happened since then.'

'Well, Mr Atkins, a man was shot in the street at 8 am this morning and we're trying to find out what happened and to see if anybody saw anything.'

His face dropped.

'Shot. In ma street. Am ah safe here? What's the world coming tae? What youz doing aboot it?'

I did my best to calm him down and asked him some more questions. But as he hadn't seen anything more than the police cars he wasn't going to be much use to the inquiry. I hoped that DS Green had had more luck.

Fortunately some of the people I interviewed after him had better information to give me, and by the end of the morning I'd gathered a lot of witness statements. Several people had heard the shot being fired, some had seen a guy in a motor-cycle helmet standing at the bus shelter, and some had seen the man who'd been murdered walking past the shelter just before the shots were fired. A few witnesses had seen the man in the motorcycle helmet walk up behind the victim and point something that resembled a gun at the back of his head at point-blank range. They knew something serious was happening because he fell straight down without putting his hands out to save himself even though he was a fit and well-built man. Others had heard a bang and seen the body slumped on the pavement. After a couple of hours of door-knocking I was pleased with the statements I'd collected.

When I met up with DS Green he was very excited because he'd interviewed a bus-driver, Jim Daldry, who had been driving past immediately after the shooting had happened. He'd been going in the opposite direction and had stopped to let the man with the motorcycle helmet cross the road. But he realized something had happened when he saw the body lying on the other side of the road so he jumped out of the bus cab and grabbed the man. The motorcyclist pointed a gun at him and shouted to him to back off. The bus-driver froze, then watched him helplessly as he got on a motorbike which was parked at the side of the road, put the gun back inside his jacket and drove off at speed towards Great Western Road.

The ballistics team had found the shell of the bullet in a field behind a wall that ran behind the bus shelter. From this they could tell that the killer had used a handgun.

We headed back to Dover Street police station to update the officer in charge of the inquiry, Superintendent Tom Bradshaw. I was still based at Williamstone but had been called to Dover Street divisional headquarters to help out. The first seventy-two hours in any murder inquiry are the 'golden' time, and everyone was buzzing around the briefing room like a particularly busy swarm of bees, exchanging newly gathered information.

We shared theories about who might have pulled the trigger and what the motive had been. Was it a revenge attack? A hired hit man? A family member? At this stage of the inquiry we kept our options open. The Serious Crime Squad had been drafted in to work on the murder. They were nicknamed the Serious Statement-Taking Squad because they had a reputation for not getting too involved in frontline crime.

An incident room had been set up with what is known as a HOLMES team to staff it – a Home Office Large Major Enquiry System. The team was a mixture of police and civilian staff specially trained to run the HOLMES computer system which links up all the information gathered and cross-references anything relevant. It identifies any gaps in the inquiry that need to be plugged. If different people have come up with inconsistent information the computer tells the officers to re-interview those witnesses or suspects.

Superintendent Bradshaw addressed the fifty officers assembled for the briefing. Because it was such a high-profile murder everybody had been drafted in. It was the first time I'd worked on such a big operation.

He ran through what was known so far. The dead man was Ralph Sprott, although many people knew him by his nickname of 'Big Ralphie'. He was thirty-four years old, a married father of one, and had worked part-time as both a fireman and a steward in a club. A man wearing a black crash helmet had shot him dead at point-blank range at a bus stop in a busy street at 8 am that morning, just yards from his home, while he was returning from his night shift.

Glasgow had plenty of fatal stabbings, but shootings, particularly ones like this, were very rare. Ralph Sprott was a martial arts expert, and he had been cleared two years before of attempting to murder his ex-partner, John Ferrier. They had been running a nightclub security firm together at the time. He had ruptured Ferrier's pancreas with a powerful kick during a row over the business but the jury had decided he'd acted in self-defence.

'The killer obviously had balls,' I said to myself, 'to shoot the guy in such a crowded area at such a busy time of the morning.'

Supt Bradshaw explained that some witness statements had come in from people who had seen the killer walk calmly back to his motorcycle that was parked across the road after the killing and drive off. This tied in with the comments from the bus-driver.

Supt Bradshaw pointed to us. 'Anne, John, what have youz found out?'

We eagerly filled him in on the statements we'd gathered. He nodded approvingly and turned to another two officers who'd also just come back into the incident room.

'How about you, Simon and Phil?'

'We spoke to a woman who gets a bus at that bus stop at the same time every morning,' said Simon excitedly. 'Her name is Beverly Norman and she noticed the suspect standing along-side her at the bus stop for a couple of days before the shooting happened. She thought it was strange because a few buses passed but he didn't get on any of them.'

'That would tie in with what I found out,' said another officer who'd been listening intently. 'I spoke to the chief fire officer, who told me that Ralph was meant to be on the night shift for the last two nights but he'd changed his shift and taken some holiday. The gunman obviously didn't know that.'

'Good work,' said the superintendent. 'Just to fill you all in, DS Blantyre took a statement from a witness who was standing at the bottom of Kilbowie Road waiting to get picked up from his work. This guy just happens to be a motorbike nerd. He knows everything about motorbikes and told us that the bike used is a black and red Honda 1,000 cc. He could even tell us that the bike has been modified and that the exhaust pipe has been changed. He said he was heading for the Erskine Bridge. This is a great breakthrough for us. We're lucky to get this information. We've got DCs Lynch and Moffatt working on the CCTV cameras on Erskine Bridge. So continue with your inquiries everyone and we'll do a briefing at 7 am tomorrow. There's unlimited overtime tonight, but try and get home and get some sleep.'

'Fill your boots,' I heard one of the DCs next to me whisper, obviously thrilled about the overtime.

I worked until about midnight on the first day of the inquiry, getting as many witness statements as I could. When I got home, about 1 am, Ali was already asleep and I fell into bed and snuggled up beside him. He was still asleep at 6 am when I had to get up and start my shift. I kissed his head tenderly. We were used to not seeing much of each other when one of us was working intensively on an inquiry. It was the nature of the job.

A few days later we got to see the photographs of Ralph's body. He was a large man and was dressed in his fireman's shirt, trousers and boots. At the back of his head was a round hole that looked completely unreal. He had no defensive injuries because he'd had no time to put up a fight. He had clearly been the victim of a premeditated, cold-blooded murder. When I saw the photos I felt a stab of pity for the family who had been expecting him home that morning but would never see him again. Seeing him photographed on the cold mortuary table really brought the situation home to me.

DS Green and I were asked to try to trace the motorbike. We carried out a Police National Computer check and narrowed down that make and model of bike to 180 in the Glasgow area. As we trawled through the list of names we also decided to check the *Auto Trader* to see if any motorbikes fitting that description were up for sale.

Other officers looked into Ralph's background. They found out more about his relationship with John Ferrier and the bad blood that existed between them. It emerged that Ralph Sprott and John Ferrier used to run a stewarding business supplying door staff to local nightclubs, and they'd had a major fall-out a couple of years earlier. Ralph Sprott had assaulted John Ferrier. Ferrier had vowed to get his revenge and had made no secret of it. This emerged in various statements. Ferrier was a suspect, but it became difficult to prove because he had gone on holiday abroad at the time of the murder.

As I looked through *Auto Trader* I found a bike for sale that was registered to Kevin Bell, a man who lived in Paisley on the other side of the Erskine Bridge. DS Green and I interviewed him and he told us he had loaned the bike to a man called James Dunn a few days before the murder. Dunn had told Bell that the bike was in a lock-up in Erskine and that if Bell sold it – which of course he was reluctant to do – Dunn would compensate him. Bell was suspicious but he was intimidated by Dunn and didn't want to ask too many questions. Although he wasn't the sharpest tool in the box, Bell became a crucial witness.

We started looking into James Dunn. He too was a body-builder, and he was associated with John Ferrier. Our inquiries revealed more links between the two of them. They trained together and were linked to each other through phone records.

An informant tipped us off about where the bike was. It was recovered in a lock-up garage near Dunn's home and identified as the bike used in the murder. Dunn's house was searched and we found clothing that matched the description seen by witnesses at the scene.

Six weeks into the inquiry evidence was beginning to mount up against James Dunn. We examined the bike, which was identified as having been modified, and Dunn was charged with the murder. I felt very proud that I had helped to track him down.

A police informant gave us a lot of information and he told us that witnesses were being intimidated. The police warned the people making the threats to stay away from the witnesses and promised the witnesses that if things got too bad they could go into witness protection. This was a big step to take, as it meant adopting a new identity and moving to a completely different area. One witness did take up the offer and started a new life somewhere else.

It was alleged that John Ferrier had paid James Dunn £5,000 to commit the murder. A search was carried out to see if any financial links could be found between the two men. A warrant was issued giving us permission to search John Ferrier's house and in his home office a lot of shredded paper was seized. My job was to piece together some of the fragments to try to prove links between Dunn and Ferrier. Painstakingly I pieced together bank statements and telephone records that named James Dunn. The link was made. John Ferrier was arrested and charged with conspiracy to murder.

James Dunn was put onto an identity parade – it was hard finding other body-builders to take part. He wasn't picked out, but later we were told by one of the witnesses that he had been warned not to pick him out. He told us he knew James Dunn because he lived in Erskine.

When the case came to court a verdict of not proven was delivered. After the heady excitement of finding enough evidence to charge James Dunn and John Ferrier with Ralph Sprott's murder, I was gutted and very frustrated.

The not proven verdict is unique to Scotland. It means that the jury is not convinced that there is enough evidence either to convict or to acquit. It reminded me of one of the first-ever cases I'd heard in a courtroom where the same thing had happened. It was 1992, the year I joined the police, and Francis Auld was charged with murdering nineteen-year-old Amanda Duffy. The police took us to Glasgow High Court to see how a serious court case was tried. It was a particularly vicious murder and the victim had a catalogue of terrible injuries including a bite to her breast. Twigs had been pushed into her orifices. I searched the face of the man accused to see if someone capable of such a terrible crime looked different from the rest of us, but he had an angelic baby face. The evidence seemed to me to be overwhelming, and although I only spent one day there I believed the testimony of the orthodontist who proved that the bite mark from the victim's breast matched the accused's tooth impressions. I was appalled when the jury returned a 'not proven' verdict. There was a public outcry, and a petition was lodged in an attempt to overturn the decision, but to no avail.

The not proven verdict was famously referred to by Sir Walter Scott as 'that bastard verdict'. I can't think of a better description for it.

# Twenty-one

One late shift, I was sitting by myself going through the daily crime log which summarizes all crimes that have happened in the last twenty-four hours. The office was deserted. Most of the day shift had gone home and it was a quiet night for crime, so there wasn't much activity.

A uniformed officer, Inspector Kenny Dunbar, strode through the swing doors into the CID office. 'There's a woman called Jean McManus in the front office. She says she's been raped,' he informed me, rolling his eyes with boredom.

'What's the story?' I asked.

'I haven't spoken to her, I'm too busy. It's probably a lot of crap.' He strolled out of the door before I got a chance to ask him anything else.

His attitude infuriated me. Like all too many of the male officers I came across, he was very dismissive about rape. A few weeks before a detective sergeant and a detective constable had been on duty when a very distressed female TV personality walked into the police station. She explained that a man had broken into her home while she was sleeping and had raped her. The officers had been scornful of her story and sent her on her way. Not prepared to accept that kind of treatment, she had put in a major complaint. Both the officers who had dealt with her were moved back to uniformed duties but no other action was taken against them. Some officers were particularly disparaging about prostitutes who reported rape, but they behaved little better towards other women who had been violated in this way.

I contacted one of the officers from the Female and Child Unit on the radio. She was out and about and I asked her to come and join me to do the interview. Then I picked up some statement paper and went out to see Jean.

The front office had its usual odour of sweat, stale cigarette smoke and urine. A ragtag collection of characters were hunched on benches in the waiting area. There was a young, spotty, skinny man wearing a baseball cap who looked as if he was a heroin addict. In his hand was a half-smoked roll-up. Next to him was an older woman with the distinctive ruddy, red-veined face of an alcoholic, and on the other side of him the woman who I presumed was Jean. She looked as if she was in her late twenties. Her head was bowed, showing two inches of black roots in her lank bleached hair. She'd tied it up in a scrunchie and the spiky ponytail was stuck up like a pineapple top. She too was skinny and was wearing a pair of oversized jogging bottoms and a food stained T-shirt which looked as if they belonged to a boyfriend. She'd applied bright blue eye shadow unevenly with a heavy hand.

Jean had struck up a conversation with the man in the baseball cap and they were sharing the roll-up. I wondered if he was her stick man – the boyfriend of a prostitute who both watches out for her and sometimes robs her punters after she lures them into back lanes.

A smart solicitor in pinstripes was also sitting on the bench, speaking into his dictaphone and clutching his shiny briefcase protectively. He looked as if he was trying to sit as far away as he could from the other three, as if any kind of body-to-body contact might contaminate him.

'Jean McManus?' I called.

The woman with the bleached hair stood up. 'That's me,' she said in a rough voice.

'How're you doing Jean? I'm DC Ramsay. Do you want to follow me?'

I led her through the back office into one of the interview rooms. As she followed me down the corridor she said in a matter-of-fact tone, 'You'd make a few bob selling your fanny.'

I said nothing. As we settled down at the table, I watched her carefully but could see none of the signs of distress or trauma that I would have expected to find in a woman who had just been raped.

'You wanted to report that you'd been raped?' I said to her gently.

'You got a fag?' she asked in her gravelly voice. I handed her the last one from the packet I kept for victims and suspects and she lit it eagerly.

'Ah've been sitting there for a fucking hour,' she complained.

I was angry that she'd been left waiting for so long and that her allegation of rape obviously hadn't been taken seriously. 'I'm sorry about that. I'm here to help you,' I said evenly.

'I came in to get my stereo,' she said. 'You bastards took

it from ma hoose three weeks ago thinking it was stolen, and I want it back.'

I was taken aback. I'd expected to be hearing a tearful account of rape. 'What's that got to do with you being raped? That's what I'm here to speak to you about.'

'Och, that was three weeks ago,' she said dismissively.

At that moment there was a knock on the door. The young female officer from the Female and Child Unit had arrived.

'Hello, I'm Constable McBride. I'm here to help DC Ramsay,' she said as she joined us at the table. I asked her if she could go and get some more cigarettes – this was going to take a while. She nodded and left the room. Then I turned back to Jean and asked, 'Can you tell me what happened?'

She took a deep drag on her cigarette. 'I picked up a punter and gave him a blow job. He said he'd give me more money for full sex so I did it. Then the bastard didnae pay me!'

'So you had consenting sex?'

'Aye, but the bastard didnae pay me,' she repeated.

'Jean, that's not rape,' I said exasperatedly. 'That was a "fail to pay" transaction.'

We often had this kind of crime reported by taxi-drivers. They picked up a passenger, requested a fare, but then the passenger jumped out of the cab without paying.

Jean didn't seem too bothered that the incident wasn't a rape. She was far more concerned about her missing stereo. Like many prostitutes who had constant dealings with the police, she was not in awe of us and had a very casual attitude towards us.

'What time is it?' she asked distractedly, taking a final drag on her cigarette before stubbing it out.

'It's 8 pm,' I replied.

'I need to go, I'm heading down to the drag. I've got money to make. I'll come back for my stereo another time.'

PC McBride bounded eagerly back into the room with a packet of cigarettes and enough statement paper to take down the whole of *War and Peace* in dictation. She looked shocked when she saw that Jean had gone.

'Where is she?' she asked.

'Oh, it was a lot of rubbish, a fail to pay. She didn't want to hang around because she had business to do.'

We walked back to the Female and Child Unit's office together.

'I get so annoyed when women like Jean come in crying rape when it hasn't happened,' I said. 'It makes it much harder for other women who have been raped to be taken seriously by the police.'

'I know,' said PC McBride. 'But I got a good result a few months ago. I arrested a punter who a prostitute had accused of raping her. It might be hard to prove but we've got a good case against him. By the way, did you hear about DS Brewster, DC Callaghan and that TV personality who was raped?'

'I know they got moved but I don't know the story,' I said.

'They told her she was lying. She was really distraught and was trying to tell them about the man who had broken into her house and raped her. They said to her, "Go away, hen, and sleep it off."'

It didn't seem to matter who the woman was who reported rape. They all appeared to be treated with equal disdain by some officers. I walked back to the CID office and began to think about my friend Julie, who was also working in the

Female and Child Unit. I wondered how she found dealing with rape allegations. I suddenly realized that I hadn't spoken to her for ages and dialled the number of her unit. The officer who answered the phone told me she had been off sick with stress for a while. I assumed she wasn't coping with the work very well. Feeling bad that we'd lost touch, I made a mental note to give her a call at home soon.

My mind drifted back to Jean McManus. She reminded me of Sharon Duncan, a girl I was at school with. We had lived a few doors away from each other and had been best pals, inseparable for a while. She had an older brother called John who was in my sister Lynne's class at school. Sharon was a pretty, striking girl with long dark hair, big brown eyes and sallow skin. She was feisty and independent, something we had in common. During the school holidays we would often meet up straight after breakfast and go off on adventures to the fields and countryside surrounding our houses. We loved playing on a rope swing over the water and then would head off to a place we called the sandy beaches. It was actually a landfill, but to us it felt like a palm-fringed beach in the Caribbean. We often didn't come home until after dark, covered in muck from head to toe. The first thing our mums did when they saw us was shove us into the bath. When we got to secondary school we grew apart, and after school I went off and did my own thing and became best pals with my cousin Lesley.

Not long after I joined the police I was shown an example of the form that was used to charge prostitutes with soliciting. I was shocked to see Sharon Duncan's name on it and I quickly checked the rest of the form. The address was near where we used to live and the description and date of birth matched hers.

The words on the form blurred as I blinked back tears. What could have gone so wrong, that the girl I had known so well had become a prostitute? Later, I found out that when she was thirteen she'd got up one morning to find that both her parents had disappeared. They'd moved abroad and left her and her brother in the house alone without telling them they were leaving.

The two children couldn't look after themselves, although they tried to for a couple of years. Their house was filthy and was infested with stray cats. Nobody seemed bothered about what was happening to them and eventually the council took the house off them. By this time Sharon was sixteen and her brother was eighteen. Sharon turned to prostitution and her brother became a rent boy. He died a few years later.

I thought of Jean again and guessed that, like Sharon, the circumstances of her life had forced her down this road. People are quick to pass judgement on women who are involved in prostitution, but the events leading to this are more complicated than they suppose. Circumstances had led Sharon into selling sex. Some of the prostitutes I met when I was patrolling the streets were not drug-users but were working in low-paid jobs like nursing and just came out at Christmas to get money to buy presents for their kids. The police were apt to make sweeping generalizations about the people they scooped up off the streets and put into police cells, generalizations that did real harm to vulnerable women like Sharon.

I picked up a newspaper that was lying around on one of the desks. 'Prostitute killer gets life' blared the headline. DC Joe Collins wandered in and read the page over my shoulder.

'That's a good result,' he said to me. He had been heavily involved in the case.

The good result that DC Collins was referring to was the jailing for life of Brian Donnelly. He had been convicted of the brutal murder of a prostitute who he had strangled in the centre of Glasgow after having sex with her in one of the lanes in the red-light district on 28 February 1998, the night of his nineteenth birthday.

He had flown into a rage after being rejected by a female colleague on a works night out, and on leaving had picked up a prostitute. He was captured on CCTV with the woman before they went off to have sex. Her battered and naked body was found the next day. The leather jacket she'd been wearing was missing from the scene and Donnelly was seen walking away in it. The prostitute had fought for her life and had scratched Donnelly hard in the face. When he turned up for work the next day with the scratches visible he told a colleague that he had been involved in a tussle with a woman whose boyfriend had tried to jump the taxi queue before him. He told another colleague that he had been scratched by a cat. One of his workmates was suspicious of his two different stories and passed his name to detectives investigating the murder.

During the trial Donnelly alleged that the murder was committed by another man, a construction worker from Scarborough who was working in Glasgow at the time. He knew, through his solicitor, that the police had suspected the construction worker of the murder before arresting him. DNA from used condoms found at the murder scene was linked to both men. However, the other man was seen on CCTV with the prostitute before she was seen with Donnelly. The other man, who had convictions for violent sex crimes against women, gave evidence and denied being the murderer. I listened to all the details of the case and felt great satisfaction about the outcome. DC Collins explained how the damning evidence had piled up against Donnelly.

I looked back at the newspaper. Calum MacNeill, the prosecuting barrister, was quoted as saying in court to Donnelly, 'We will never know why you killed her, whether it was a disagreement over payment or your anger which lacks self-control or out of shame or disgust or contempt that you had for the heroin-addicted prostitute you had just used.

'You punched and kicked her and she fought back, scratching you. You were incensed, you six foot three inches tall and her only five foot. You were fuelled with anger and got out of control and banged her head off the wall before strangling her and finally dragging her body along the yard.'

The prostitute's mother was also quoted in the article saying, 'She might have been a prostitute but she was still a lovely lassie with a heart of gold.'

The prostitute was Margo Lafferty.

# Twenty-two

Hyndland is a sought-after area of Glasgow populated by young urban professionals who inhabit the city's fashionable red stone tenement buildings. It wasn't an area that we needed to go to very often, but early one morning we were called to a flat in one of its elegant streets. An old woman who lived in the flat opposite had been awoken at 6 am by a knock on the door. She lived alone and the knocking frightened her, but all the same she put on her dressing gown and opened the door.

She could not believe what she saw, and clapped her hand over her mouth in horror. Crouched on all fours was a naked man wearing a gimp mask – a tight leather mask with holes for the eyes and a zip over the mouth. He was moaning in pain. Blood had soaked through the mask at the back of his head. The old woman cried out, shut the door and dialled 999. She did not recognize the man as her usually sober-suited neighbour, a university professor.

I was one of the first CID officers on the scene, decked out in my teletubbies suit so that I could gather forensic evidence without contaminating it. By the time I arrived the professor had been rushed to hospital with serious head injuries. Uniformed officers who were on the scene before me told me he was unconscious when he was carried out, so no one had been able to question him about what had happened. I walked through the beautiful stained-glass front door into the professor's flat. It was immaculately clean and furnished in a tasteful traditional style.

The bedroom, though, looked completely different. It was as if an entirely separate part of this man's life was contained here. Heavy green velour curtains were tightly drawn. The gimp mask was still at the scene. Presumably the ambulance staff had removed it from his head when they arrived. I picked it up and placed it in a bag, as it would be a key piece of evidence. It was heavy with blood which had turned the black leather a deep shade of burgundy. I recoiled as I saw clumps of hair and bits of what I presumed were the man's skull stuck to the inside of the mask. A shiver went down my spine as I tried to imagine what had happened. Judging by the amount of his head stuck to the inside of the mask I was sure we would be dealing with a murder.

Once the mask was bagged up I took a closer look around. I could see every imaginable sex toy in the room, some on the chest of drawers, others on top of the wardrobe and under the bed. Some were easily identifiable – whips, nipple clamps, vibrators and various phallic-shaped objects – but others I had never seen before and had no idea how they could be used. I laughed grimly when I found what I presumed were 'ball weights' which could be attached to testicles. There were two forensics officers in the flat too, and one of them picked up a marble pyramid with grooves on it.

'What the hell is that?' asked one of the officers.

I shrugged. I'd never come across anything like it before. I began searching the room for a weapon and found a blood-stained Irn Bru bottle, which I carefully placed in an evidence bag. Postcards from Amsterdam and bits of paper with phone numbers on also went into evidence bags.

The bed had crumpled sheets on it that I removed. I noticed that there were silk restraints tied to the corners of the head-board where presumably the professor had been tied up. We took these as evidence, along with any of the heavier sex toys that might conceivably have been the murder weapon.

I headed back to the CID office with my haul. News of the crime had spread around the office, and because of its unusual nature everyone was agog to know what I'd found. I described the gruesome scene and asked if anyone could enlighten me as to the function of some of the weirder devices.

Although I joked with my colleagues about some of the sex toys, I was very disturbed by the blood-sodden gimp mask and couldn't get it out of my mind.

I found out from other officers that despite my prediction that he wouldn't survive the attack, the professor had regained consciousness but said he didn't want to make any complaint. Checks had been made on his phone records and it was dis-covered that he had contacted a rent boy called James McAlvin the night before. We managed to find McAlvin very quickly, tracing him to his home address in a high-rise flat in Glasgow's rundown Gorbals area. CCTV evidence showed him returning home covered in blood, and we discovered he'd been telling people he was terrified he'd killed the professor.

McAlvin was a skinny young man who offered no resist-

ance when officers went to arrest him at his home. He freely
admitted having been with the professor and explained to the
officers who interviewed him what had happened. According
to him he'd got a call on his mobile from the professor at
around 8 pm the previous night asking him if he'd meet him
for sex. He agreed and was picked up by the professor in
Kelvin Way around 10 pm.

Kelvin Way was a well-known gay haunt. The two men had
gone back to the professor's flat and had had sex.

'Then he started asking for more kinky things. I'm not gay
but I wanted the money to buy drugs so I went along with it.'
McAlvin was tearful as he told the story. He wasn't known for
violence and seemed genuinely upset by what had happened.

'The professor asked me to tie him up and to use different
kinds of weird sex toys on him. He kept wanting to change
outfits and ended up naked with a gimp mask on. While the
professor was lying face down on the bed and I was on top of
him having sex with him he told me I wasn't going to get paid.

'I was very angry. I'd been there for a long time and had
had to do these disgusting things to him. Then he told me
he had no money so I picked up an Irn Bru bottle and
started bashing him on the back of the head with the base of
it. At first the professor seemed to be enjoying it, but when I
saw all the blood I got scared, ran out of the flat and went
home.'

We found about £400 cash in professor's house, so we
wondered why he would say this when he obviously did have
money. Maybe he'd been planning to pay, but got off on the
physical pain that McAlvin's anger had caused him to inflict.
It seemed a strange thing for the boy to lie about. I thought

that McAlvin would probably have a good defence because the professor obviously liked pain. I was moved on to another case and never got to find out what happened to McAlvin.

Prostitution is often policed in fits and starts, and no matter what initiatives police take to tackle the problem, sex continues to be sold. Every now and then, senior officers would decide that it was time to carry out a raid on a particular sauna or brothel, or on several at once. Sometimes this was in response to political pressure, at other times to a string of complaints from local residents. I'm not sure what was behind the decision to raid one of Glasgow's biggest saunas, but an edict from senior officers took ten of us plain-clothed officers there to get evidence that not just massages but also a full range of sexual services were for sale, so that we could close the place down. We were also told to find out if there were any illegal immigrants working there. We were keen to discover who was running the place in case they had links to organized crime.

Most of us went in through the front door and a couple were stationed at the back. I'd never been inside a sauna before and wasn't sure what to expect. We pushed open the door and found ourselves in the plush hallway of an old Victorian townhouse. The smell of cheap pot-pourri hit my nose, and I noted the thick shagpile carpet on the floor. A pleasant-looking plump blonde woman sat behind a desk. A huge commotion broke out when everyone realized they were being raided. We quickly barged into the seven bedrooms calling out, 'Police! Get dressed.'

Some of the women were fuming at the intrusion. 'I'm not

doing anything wrong,' a couple of them protested to the officers.

The sauna was on three floors and women were running around in all directions and in various states of undress. There were twelve girls altogether, and we gathered them in the lounge. Men who'd been caught *in flagrante* hurried down the stairs, hastily pulling on their shirts and zipping up their trousers. Some had towels round them.

I was one of two female officers there and we were quite amused by the whole thing. The male officers' eyes were popping out of their heads. They kept nudging and winking at each other each time they saw yet another voluptuous young woman. They were in their element.

The bedrooms had different themes. One was a 'tiger room' with jungle prints on the walls and a cheap polyester duvet on the bed with pictures of tigers on it. There was a dungeon room painted completely black with various pieces of bondage equipment and TVs everywhere playing porn movies. 'Ooh' and 'Ahh' sounds from the films echoed around the place.

Used as I was to dealing with prostitutes who worked on the streets, I couldn't believe how different these women were. Many of them were the kind of woman you'd see in the school playground, and indeed some of them were mothers who were doing this work because the hours were flexible and they could fit it in around their childcare commitments. The women came from various different continents – Africa, Asia and various parts of Europe, particularly eastern Europe. All of them seemed very together, they earned good money from what they did and took pride in their work.

There appeared to be a real camaraderie between the girls. They were protective of each other and were very complimentary about the owner of the sauna and their working conditions. They all knew what they were supposed to say and were emphatic about the fact that they were only providing massages. There were five customers there when we arrived. They were separated from the women and interviewed by the male officers.

Some of the male customers had been less well briefed and admitted they were here to have sex with the women. The male officers put pressure on them by saying, 'Maybe we should speak to you about this in the presence of your wife.'

I thought about how many male officers cheated on their wives. The officers were behaving very self-righteously towards the male customers and the inconsistency of their stance never crossed their minds.

We detained the blonde woman behind the desk despite her protests.

'This is ridiculous. I'm running a legitimate business,' she said. 'I want to call the owner.'

The senior officer in charge of the operation decided to shut the place down for the night so that more inquiries could be made. The owner of the brothel was eventually charged. Even though there were semi-naked women running around everywhere he insisted that no sex was being sold from his premises, but he was convicted of living off immoral earnings. He received a six-month jail sentence.

When police raid premises like these they are always portrayed as enforcers of some kind of moral code. However, a colleague told me later that when the credit-card receipts of men who had purchased services at the sauna were examined it emerged that one of the visitors was a senior police officer. Soon afterwards he was moved sideways to a boring desk job. His indiscretion never became public.

# Twenty-three

'So tell me more about your relationship with Ali,' said Dr Arbuthnot. I was sitting in my usual chair in her consulting room. I'd been coming here twice a week for the last four months and was starting to feel more relaxed. The fading afternoon light cast long shadows across her polished wooden floorboards. At the mention of Ali's name a wave of sadness washed over me.

'I loved him to bits,' I said. 'He made me laugh. We had a great relationship. I'm sorry, what else do you want to know?'

'Were you close, did you talk?'

'When we were first together we talked all the time, we were inseparable. We could talk for hours about anything and everything.'

I could feel myself getting upset again just remembering how good things had been between us.

'You were both police officers. Did you work together?'

'No, we had totally different jobs. Ali was in the community police and worked in a different area from me. He was a trained firearms officer. I was in the CID. He seemed to look up to me because I was a detective. I had a lot of respect for him because he'd been a paramedic in Belfast before he joined the police and could tell stories that would make your hair curl. Some of the things he'd seen before made the police look like Disneyland.

'I never really felt that we were both in the police when we were together because our focus was on our lives outside the police. Our jobs were very different. He was the youngest trained firearms officer in Strathclyde Police. He came from a loving family, as I did, and he had grown up in Ireland. Both of us shared the same strong family values.'

Dr Arbuthnot nodded encouragingly.

'Did the police have an effect on your lives?'

'Not at the beginning because we had so much in common away from the job. We were both really sporty and went to the gym together. We used to take my nieces and nephews out together. The kids used to call Ali The Rock because he looked like The Rock on WWF.'

I was feeling animated at the thought of all the things Ali and I had done together.

'He was good at impersonations and used to phone my mum up pretending to be other people. He really made everyone laugh. He was the life and soul of the party.'

'When did you stop talking?'

'We fell in love with a house in a nice area. It was a detached bungalow. An old woman had been living in it for years, so it needed some updating. We both needed to sell our flats to be able to afford to buy the house and were bidding against eight other people to buy it. My flat sold quickly but Ali's didn't, so we ended up with a bridging loan that lasted for a year, and that put a huge strain on our relationship. I stopped talking to him and whenever he tried to broach the subject of our debt I snapped at him. I wasn't dealing with our debt problems and stuck my head in the sand. The less money we had the more I spent. We had no money to go out and do the normal things couples do like going to restaurants and the cinema, so to console myself I indulged in covert retail therapy, buying clothes then hiding them from him. I was in denial and kept thinking, "Things will get better, things will get better." Every time Ali tried to talk to me about it I refused to listen. He was trying to hold everything together and that was putting a strain on him.'

Dr Arbuthnot nodded understandingly.

'We hardly knew each other. We had only been together for three months when we decided to buy a house together. I was madly in love with him but we should have given the relationship time to grow. I should have talked to Ali but I just didn't deal with things very well.'

'Do you normally do that?'

'I'm the type of person who can handle everybody else's problems but I don't really speak to anyone about my own.'

'You know, when you do that people don't realize you need help. When you're helping people all the time they would love for you to ask them for help. It would make them feel good. By not asking for help you're not being good to yourself. Would you say this was a real low point in your life?'

'Yes, but then things got even worse. My mum nearly died.'

'Can you tell me about that?'

'Mum started to get breathless and went a terrible ashen colour. Very quickly she changed from being a person who was very well to one who was very ill. I took her down to

Casualty. They gave her a chest X-ray but said they could find nothing wrong and sent her home. I knew something wasn't right and took her to see the GP. He couldn't find anything wrong with her either and sent her away with asthma inhalers, but she collapsed on her way out of the surgery. "I know I'm not a doctor," I shouted, "but she can't breathe, something's wrong."'

I tried to continue but I was sobbing too much.

'If you're not ready we can speak next week. You're doing very well,' said Dr Arbuthnot.

'It's OK,' I said in a shaky voice. 'Maybe I need to get it out. She was rushed to hospital and this time a chest X-ray revealed that there was a huge shadow close to her heart. Whoever had read the X-ray the previous week when she'd been in Casualty had completely missed it. Her blood pressure was very low and she kept on going into cardiac arrest. She was started on Heparin to thin the blood, and without that I don't know what would have happened.

'My mum was in a critical condition and remained in that state for forty-eight hours. We all kept a vigil around her bedside. We were told that a professor who was an expert surgeon was away for the weekend but was back on Monday and would carry out some exploratory surgery on her. The doctors had a serious talk to the family and told us that Mum was very ill and might not survive. I was very close to my mum and the thought of losing her was devastating. When the professor operated on her he found a clot that they told us was a pulmonary embolism, the size of the palm of a hand, blocking the vein into her heart. He managed to scoop a lot of it out but she remained in a critical condition for two days. The pressure in Mum's lungs was dangerously high and the doctors had to do everything they could to bring it down. We were told that her chances of survival were only about 20 per cent.'

Dr Arbuthnot looked at me sympathetically. 'You must have been under a huge amount of stress,' she said quietly. I nodded and gulped back tears.

'My mum did survive. The doctors couldn't believe it and she was written up in the medical textbooks – most people would not have lived through a clot like that. I was overjoyed, of course, that she'd come through it. She was in hospital for three more weeks and I went to visit her at home the day she was discharged. I sat down on the sofa and was suddenly struck by a crippling pain in my chest. I went a horrible shade of grey and clutched my chest. I couldn't breathe and I thought I was going to die.

'"There's something wrong, there's something wrong," I cried, convinced that I too had a clot which was lodged in my heart and that if I moved even a millimetre from my position slumped on the sofa it would travel to my brain. Ali was with me and he kept telling me to calm down. My mum was distraught. She was weeping and saying over and over again, "This is terrible. This is terrible, I hope it isn't because of me." An ambulance was called and I was taken to Western Infirmary. I was given oxygen in the ambulance and that made me feel a bit better. At the hospital the doctors asked me if I'd been suffering from stress and exhaustion. I said I had and they diagnosed a panic attack.'

'When did the panic attacks start?' asked Dr Arbuthnot.

'That was the first one. I had them regularly after that and found I couldn't sleep.'

'What did the doctor say about it?'

'She said I was exhausted and had to get more sleep, and get fit again. She prescribed me a low dose of diazepam for a short time to help me sleep, but I didn't like that. I woke up every morning feeling as if I'd been hit over the head with a hammer. Other than that I was told to blow into a paper bag if I had an attack, and when I felt it starting I needed to concentrate on taking deep breaths and try not to let the attack take over. In the end she signed me off work for four weeks, for stress and anxiety.'

'Did Ali help you with the panic attacks you suffered?' she asked, glancing at the clock. I couldn't believe how fast the hour had gone.

'He tried to, but he began to have problems of his own and they affected me too.'

'Let's talk about that next week,' said Dr Arbuthnot.

# Twenty-four

'So,' said Dr Arbuthnot, 'tell me what happened.'

'Ali was marked down in an appraisal by his supervisor for his poor communication skills and his judgement. He was a good police officer and was devastated by this.

'I said to him, "That doesn't sound right, you're a firearms officer. How can they mark you down for judgement when they've given you a gun, and how can they say you can't communicate when you're a community officer?"

'A lot of his problems seemed to stem from a particular officer called Sergeant Graves. Ali felt that the sergeant left him out of things and passed him over for various jobs. I urged Ali to challenge his appraisal. When Ali told him he wasn't happy about it, Sergeant Graves just said, "Too bad." After that Ali felt that he was treated even worse because he had dared to challenge his boss. So he went above him and spoke to Chief Inspector Mike Thompson, who backed up Sergeant Graves and told him his appraisal was staying the same. Ali took it further and went to see the deputy divisional commander, who agreed with him that his appraisal was unfair. He assured him he would sort things out and also said that he respected Ali, thought he was a good officer and would be able to get his marks changed.

'But that never happened because he went off on holiday and Chief Inspector Thompson stepped in to cover for him. That's when things got much worse. He got Ali moved to a different office and served him with disciplinary papers. "Under no circumstances are your marks getting changed," he told Ali.'

'How did Ali cope with all this?' Dr Arbuthnot got up to turn on the lights because it was getting very dark in the room.

'He was a good police officer. He just wanted to do well at his job. He was ambitious and was very distressed by it all because he knew he'd done nothing wrong. Appraisals stay on your record throughout your career and can affect your chances of promotion.'

'What happened then?'

'Ali made a formal complaint to personnel, and then things started to get really out of hand. It was something that could have been sorted out very quickly and easily but the police allowed things to escalate. He was served with seventeen charges of neglect of duty for things like not writing crime reports up properly.'

Dr Arbuthnot raised her eyebrows.

'The kinds of things they criticized him for were estimating that it would cost £80 to repair a smashed car window when in fact the price at the local repair place was £100.'

'Did that have an impact on you?'

'I felt terrible for him. I hadn't been coping very well because of my mum and our debt and this was yet another stress to deal with. Then the police turned on me too.

'Both of us were under an enormous amount of pressure. One morning Ali came upstairs ashen-faced. I was in bed because I'd come in off my CID nightshift a few hours before. "Look at this," he said trembling. He took a piece of A4 white paper out of a brown envelope with a plastic window on the front. It had been sent to his old address and been redirected. The letter referred to his complaint to the police and said things like, "How dare you make a complaint against Sergeant Graves, he's a nice guy. Get back to where you came from, you shouldn't be in this job." I was horrified that he'd received something so racist and my first reaction was to preserve the evidence.

'We were both distraught and talked over what we should do. I had been half asleep but this jolted me awake. I think the police expected us to back off now. I'm sure it was a punishment for Ali for daring to challenge his poor appraisal. I was shocked that things had gone this far and could see how devastated Ali was. He had thought he was well liked and the depth of the hatred stunned him. I knew that if we reported it things would get even worse for him. But if we kept quiet it felt as if we were condoning something that was so obviously wrong. In the end we decided that we would make a complaint to the Commission for Racial Equality because we didn't trust the police enough and thought they might make the letter go "missing".

'We made an appointment at the CRE and spoke to one of the senior staff there whose name was Julia Hanson. She was an older woman and she listened sympathetically when we explained what had happened.

'When she'd read through the letter she sighed and said,

"We cannae have this sort of thing going on, especially from the police. You know the police come on courses here to learn about racism. They should be above this sort of thing."

'She told us she'd report it to the police right away and that she would raise a crime report. She offered to put Ali in touch with other people who had been through the same thing.

'As we walked out of the CRE office we felt that at least we had some back-up because an outside agency was involved. We felt a bit more protected from a police backlash and were more confident that our complaint would be taken seriously. But we were still anxious about what would happen to us because we'd raised our heads above the parapet. I knew the police wouldn't be happy and would regard what we'd done as an act of disloyalty. I was working night shifts at the time and felt on edge when I was in the police office.

'It was as if I was in a bad dream that I couldn't wake up from. First our debt, then my mum's illness, and now this. The misery was relentless and I felt our relationship was starting to fall apart.

'A few days later there was a knock on the door. I opened it and recognized Detective Inspector Brady because I'd worked with him before. He was with Detective Chief Inspector Harlow, who I didn't know. Detective Inspector Brady behaved formally, as if he'd never seen me before, and introduced himself. I felt my heart racing and wondered what they were going to do or say. Once inside they were brusque and I felt intimidated by the fact they were senior CID officers and I was only a detective constable. They would cut me off in midsentence and didn't seem to take me seriously. "Can you tell me how the inquiry's going?" I asked timidly.

'Detective Chief Inspector Harlow barked, "What's it got to do with you?"

'"It's got everything to do with me. The letter's been sent to my house." I looked over to Ali for support. I could see he looked hurt for me.

'"I just want this dealt with," Ali said firmly.

'I felt like bursting into tears but tried to stay composed. I didn't want to give them the satisfaction of seeing how upset I was.

'Under normal circumstances I would have offered them tea, but today social niceties were the last thing on my mind. They asked if they could take away our computer, implying that we had written the letter ourselves.

'"There's no way you're taking my computer. What are you insinuating?" asked Ali. They didn't reply but agreed to take away a piece of paper with something printed on it so that they could analyse the paper and the ink. Both of us couldn't wait for them to leave our house. We felt as if we'd been visited by the enemy and violated in some way.'

I paused for breath.

'Go on,' said Dr Arbuthnot. I started weeping.

'Ali informed them that he was going home to see his family in Ireland for a few days. About 7 am one morning when he was away and I was in the house by myself, the door-bell rang. I was half asleep and answered in my pyjamas. The same two officers were at the door. Because I had felt intimidated by their last visit, now I felt even more vulnerable. And I knew that they knew that Ali was away for the weekend.

'"We need to speak to you," said DCI Harlow abruptly. I felt that something quite serious was going to happen. Standing in the middle of the living room in my pyjamas I felt naked and asked if I could get dressed.

'"No," they said. "It won't take long." When we went into the living room they brought out what I recognized to be a DNA kit and fingerprint ink. They told me they were taking samples to eliminate me from their inquiries into the letter.'

'What did you say? How did you cope?' asked Dr Arbuthnot, her brow furrowed.

'I felt weak. I couldn't cope at all. I couldn't believe what was happening to me. I was in complete shock and felt trapped, terrified that I was being set up.

'I didn't give the samples willingly, but at the same time I knew I had no choice but to comply because I didn't want to give them a reason not to investigate the letter. And I knew I had nothing to hide.

'I felt completely bullied. This was the time of day that police officers would raid a suspected criminal's house. I couldn't believe they were treating me the same way, particularly when they knew I was off work with stress. I'd had to call on a police officer at home in the past, and had phoned first to find out when a convenient time would be. The officer's welfare came first, but in this case it seemed mine certainly didn't.

'After they'd taken the prints DI Brady said, "We need to talk to Ali but we can't tell you what it's about."

'"I can get him to call you," I said.

'"No, we need to speak to him in person. It's about another woman and we also want to interview his previous girlfriends." I knew this would be a pointless line of inquiry. Because of the information contained in the letter it could only have been written by a serving police officer.'

'How did that make you feel?' asked Dr Arbuthnot.

'I trusted Ali a hundred per cent. We were with each other all the time. I felt this was just another tactic to hurt us. I'd spoken to Ali the day before and he'd told me that they were trawling through old records of people he'd arrested, even for minor crimes, to see if they'd written the letter.'

'And how did you feel about that?'

'It made me very angry.'

'Why?' she asked.

'Because I felt that they were doing everything possible to avoid investigating themselves, even though the letter so obviously came from the police. It referred to the complaint Ali had made to the police and even mentioned the name of the senior police officer he'd complained about. Who would know that unless they were in the police?

'I called Ali after they'd gone. He was furious and phoned the police office and got an undertaking from them that all future meetings would take place at the offices of the Commission for Racial Equality.'

'What happened with the complaint?'

'Ali was determined to see it through, but the police were dragging their feet with the investigation. We had several meetings with Julia at the CRE. Senior police officers including the assistant chief constable attended some of them. The assistant chief constable shot me down when I asked what action was being taken about Ali's grievance and the letter. He said that the senior officers Ali had discussed his appraisal with had been spoken to, had apologized and had suggested that a new appraisal could be done. I asked him, "How can Ali go on working with these people when he believes they've made up all these charges against him?"

'He snapped at me and said, "How dare you question me!" He asked Ali what he wanted. "I want fairness," said Ali quietly.

'Because the police had issued seventeen charges against him on matters like the report writing he was due to go to a disciplinary hearing. Nothing was really resolved about the letter or about Ali's grievance against the police, but things seemed to be snowballing against Ali. The police were determined to get him to the disciplinary hearing. Ali had had a lot of meetings with his lawyer beforehand. Dates kept on being made and broken for these hearings. I was never cited as a witness at any of them.

'I was back at work by then and had submitted a holiday request form. With all the different stresses I'd been under I decided to take my mum to Spain for a week to recuperate from her illness. Whilst I was away on holiday the police set a date for the disciplinary hearing, and the night before they sent a DS round to my mum's house to cite me as a witness. This was strange for a couple of reasons: firstly because they hadn't allowed me to live at my mum's and I had my own home with Ali, and secondly because they knew I was away on holiday.'

'It all seems very underhand,' said Dr Arbuthnot.

'It gets worse. Ali went to the hearing. He was told to appear in full dress uniform and to wait outside the room until an inspector appeared to escort him in. He was made to march into the room and to salute the chief superintendent who sat at the top end of a large table. The charges against him were read out and then he was given permission to sit down.

'On one side of the table sat three people from the Complaints and Discipline department. Ali sat at the other side with his Police Federation lawyer and federation representative, Inspector McLelland.

'The hearing began and the police accused me of deliberately avoiding coming along and plotting to go on holiday so that the hearing couldn't go ahead. Had I been able to reply, I would have pointed out that I hadn't been called to give evidence for any of the previous cancelled hearings and had no reason to believe I would be called for this one as I could not see how I was relevant to the proceedings: the charges against Ali related to his workplace and I worked somewhere else.

'These hearings are not popular with police officers. The police have total control over the proceedings and the outcome. Ali was so sickened by the whole thing and by the way they'd treated him that he decided he no longer wanted to be part of that organization. He knew that if he did carry on in the police this would always be hanging over him and would affect his career.

'"I'm resigning," said Ali in the disciplinary hearing. "I feel as if a wall of lies has been built against me and I don't think that I can work for this organization any more."

'The police were furious because they wanted to have their day in their makeshift court. They had hoped to discredit Ali to take attention away from the issue of the letter. But even though he had resigned they still wanted to try to bring him back to discipline him. Ali's lawyer said this was ludicrous. What else could they do to him? He'd resigned!

'Inspector McClelland told Ali to tell me to watch my back. Ali called me in Spain to tell me what had happened at the hearing and to pass on Inspector McClelland's message. I shivered when I heard this but I tried to make the best of the holiday for my mum's sake. I was heartbroken for Ali, knowing how much he'd loved being a policeman and how his dreams had been shattered. But I was glad that he was out of this horrible situation that had made him so unhappy. I started to feel more and more scared that they were going to come after me.

'When I got back from Spain and went back to the office the first thing I found was that my holiday form had gone missing from my office. I couldn't find it anywhere. I decided to conduct my own investigation into the whole situation and asked the officer who had gone to my mum's house, someone I worked with, why he had done that.

'"I was told to do it," he said.

'I was furious and knew that I was being set up. I went to see Inspector McClelland and told him about my concerns and about how my holiday form had gone missing. He told me I was right to be concerned and that I should watch my back because he felt that something untoward might happen to me.'

'What was your state of mind after that meeting?' asked Dr Arbuthnot.

'On the outside I appeared to be coping but inside I felt as if I was dying. Every day something else seemed to happen and my relationship with Ali was adversely affected. My job had always been stressful, but now it was ten times worse because the stress was coming from within the police. Ali and I were both good at our jobs, but I felt it didn't matter how good we were. The police had taken against me for a reason that was nothing to do with how I did my job, and the strain of that was so much worse than the stress of dealing with any arrest or violent criminal. I was tormented by the fear of the unknown and increasingly understood how powerful they were and how powerless I was. This wasn't just a normal job that I could be sacked from. I became paranoid that the police could plant drugs on me or do something equally awful that would land me in jail. There would be absolutely nothing I could do about it. The police had total control of my life, and they could put an end to my career, and my future, whenever they wanted.

'Then Ali and I split up.'

# Twenty-five

I looked forlornly around my new home, a small, modern house in Milngavie, a well-to-do Glasgow suburb that was a twenty-minute drive from my parents' house.

There was no dramatic break-up between Ali and me. We'd more or less stopped communicating with each other because of the stress of everything that had happened to us. Our conversations were reduced to small talk and we never discussed what was happening to us or how we really felt. We were both exhausted, all our emotional energy was spent and we had nothing left to give each other. Neither of us wanted to let go of the other, but Ali wanted to go home to Ireland so that his family could support him after everything he'd been through in the police.

He toyed with the idea of going home for about six months, then decided that he was going to do it. I understood how he felt and didn't blame him for wanting to leave Scotland. I felt lonely when I was with him but this increased enormously after he left. I helped him to pack up and we agreed to continue the relationship long-distance. I went over to see him in Ireland a few times, but after six months the relationship fizzled out. It had been crushed by the weight of events.

My new place was very bare, because Ali had taken a lot of the furniture with him when we'd split up. A settee I'd ordered wasn't due to arrive for another ten weeks and so I was sitting on the floor, my knees hugged to my chest, feeling very alone. I could hear the phone ringing but didn't want to speak to anyone. I felt tired all the time and even the simplest task was a huge effort. The ringing stopped, then started again almost immediately, as if the caller knew that I was at home and was deliberately not answering. Sighing, I hauled myself up and walked across the room to where the phone was.

'Hello,' I said quietly.

It was my mum. 'Is that you, Anne?'

Normally I would have laughed and said, 'Who else could it be?' but I just breathed, 'Uh huh,' barely above a whisper.

'I've been trying to get you for days. Why haven't you been in touch?'

'I've been busy,' I said flatly.

'It's not like you not to call. Are you OK?'

'Fine,' I said. I didn't have the energy to make my voice sound cheerful.

'You don't sound like yourself,' my mum said.

'I'm just tired,' I said. I couldn't wait to get off the phone. Soon afterwards it rang again but I didn't pick it up. I sat on the floor as the light faded, thought about making myself something to eat or going for a bath, but didn't have the energy.

I'd been off work for a few days and the knowledge that I

had to go back the following day filled me with dread. I was still working at Williamstone CID and, feeling paranoid, I was constantly looking over my shoulder. I seemed to be permanently holding my breath and waiting. Just waiting.

'They probably won't do anything right away, but it's just a matter of time,' I thought to myself. My hands clenched more tightly around my knees and I watched my knuckles go white. When I finally got myself to bed I spent almost the entire night tossing and turning, finally dropping off around 6 am.

The alarm kept buzzing and finally I dragged myself out of bed at 6.45 am, feeling terrible. I didn't have the energy to have a shower or a proper wash so just splashed some water on my face and tied my greasy hair up in a ponytail. I couldn't remember the last time I'd washed it. My shirt was crumpled but I pulled a sweater on over it to hide it then left the house without eating any breakfast and drove to work.

I was in a daze and I don't remember the journey at all. I didn't jolt back into reality until I walked into Williamstone office. I was immediately told to go to Kingston Road sub-office because there'd been a serious assault and an incident room had been set up there.

I drove the short distance to Kingston Road, and as I parked I could see the place was crowded with cars, a sure sign of trouble. I sighed as I locked my car door, wanting nothing more than to get home and crawl back under the duvet.

There was a hum of conversation about whatever major incident we were here for. Usually I would have been eagerly asking what it was, but today I stayed quiet and found out soon enough by listening. A forty-year-old businessman called

Alexander Blue had been brutally attacked. He was in hospital and wasn't expected to live.

Blue had lived in an upmarket flat in Glasgow's west end and had suffered a vicious assault outside his house in the early hours of the morning. Later in the day we got information that he had received a phone call, possibly from someone he knew, which caused him to leave the house. He had then gone outside to the carport at the side of his house where his Porsche Boxter car was parked. It was there that he was attacked.

The police office was in chaos because nothing had yet been properly set up.

I was sent with another DC, Derek Harvey, to Blue's business premises, a taxi centre. He ran a business providing Skoda cars for private hire taxi-drivers. Volkswagen had bought Skoda and so the cars now had good engines, but they still suffered from a 'Soviet' image problem. It seemed that Blue was single-handedly rehabilitating the Skoda brand. He had found a gap in the market and business was booming.

Derek Harvey had a reputation for being a good DC. He could be quite abrasive and sometimes rubbed people up the wrong way, but he was very thorough, and once he got stuck into a case he was like a dog with a bone. His hair flopped over his eyes, making him look boyish even though he was in his forties. He was a very popular detective and his enthusiasm for the case perked me up.

When we arrived at Blue's premises we got a frosty reception from the manager. Derek didn't help matters by putting him in his place several times. When the manager said he wanted to call Blue's business partner midway through the conversation Derek said sharply, 'Forget it, you're not doing anything until you've answered our questions.'

I still had a strong sense of duty and a determination to act in a professional way. I tried to stifle my feelings of intense misery because I didn't want to let Derek down. But in truth my heart wasn't in what I was doing, and when I started asking questions I lacked my usual spark. Alex Blue had had a diary on his desk that could have provided vital clues to who his attacker was, but in the chaos there was a delay in seizing it and it could have been tampered with before we took it. The staff at his office clammed up when we tried to speak to them and seemed keen to make contact with Blue's business partner. That day I worked until almost 3 am. I never stopped for a break and didn't eat anything. I had gone into robot mode. The next day I started work at 8 am and the whole process began again.

Two days later Blue died of his injuries. The pathologist could not tell whether one or two weapons had been used. The wounds came from both a blunt and a sharp instrument, so he could have been attacked with a claw hammer or an ice pick. We never found the weapon and there was no DNA at the scene, which is very unusual. A neighbour reported hearing something that sounded like a fence post being hammered in ten times. The description was quite graphic and matched the injuries, which were all to his head. If Blue had been killed by a professional hit man it seemed like a strange way to do it, because this was such a slow method.

For the next few weeks I was working fourteen-hour shifts and sometimes was in the office on my days off too. I seemed to be involved in every aspect of the murder. A financial investigation was launched because Blue was a bank-rupt, despite having the Skoda business. We got in touch with Interpol because we found out he had made a trip to Cyprus, where he had apparently met some members of the Russian mafia.

We pursued many different lines of inquiry, yet none of them led anywhere. However, we did discover that there was a dispute amongst members of his family over who'd been left what in Blue's will. His brother also worked for the taxi firm, and not long after the murder Blue's business partner sacked him, which seemed strangely insensitive. Numerous criminal names came into the inquiry, but again they led nowhere.

Blue was believed to have been in a cafe called Bean Scene a few hours before he died and had possibly had a meal in a restaurant nearby. We seized as much CCTV as we could. A black BMW was identified on some of the footage, which could possibly have been the murderer fleeing Blue's house after the murder, but the quality of the film was too grainy to pick out a number plate.

I walked into the HOLMES room that had been set up at the start of the murder inquiry and spoke to Lucy, one of the civilian workers. She was typing statements into her computer.

'Can you give me a copy of a statement?' I asked.

'Who's it from?'

'The accountant Lawrence Menzies. I have to interview Blue's lawyer and I need a copy of that statement to cross-reference information.'

She leafed through the pile of papers on her desk and said, 'No, it's not here. Are you sure you submitted it?'

I started feeling panicked because I was convinced I had.

I got a sick feeling in my stomach and ran into my office to check my paperwork. I started throwing paper around, frantically trying to locate the statement. I would get into serious trouble if I couldn't find it, because it was a crucial statement and I'd spent hours taking it.

It wasn't on my desk. I put my head in my hands. 'What've I done with it?' I asked myself. My head felt fuzzy and confused and I started gasping for air. I clutched my chest. I could feel another panic attack coming on. I'd started to get these attacks almost every week. I tried to calm myself down by regulating my breathing rather than letting it overwhelm me. Then when I had pulled myself together I went to the locker room to see if I'd left the statement in my locker. I rummaged through my coat pockets and my handbag. There was a pile of memos and printed-out e-mails on the shelf, but the statement wasn't there.

'Oh my God,' I said to myself. An ominous thought had occurred to me. What if I hadn't lost the statement at all? What if it had been deliberately removed to get me into trouble?

It was all starting again. I decided it was too much of a coincidence after my annual leave form had gone missing. Enough time had passed for them to come after me. I thought about how they would try and make it seem unrelated to Ali. It had been a while since he'd left the force.

Then Lucy popped her head round the door.

'Found it,' she said. 'Someone had put it in a different tray.'

The relief was overwhelming. I felt I could breathe again, but I was still shaking.

I headed out to get a statement from the lawyer. In the course of this inquiry I'd interviewed lots of lawyers, accountants and businessmen who had links with Blue. It was very unusual to have to interview so many professionals. Most murder inquiries involved ordinary working-class people as witnesses or suspects.

Many of these professionals seemed to have something to hide, and were cagy when I took their statements. This really bothered me and I started to wonder if anyone was honest. These people were supposed to be pillars of society, but they seemed to be more driven by money and power than by doing the right thing.

At the end of yet another long, exhausting day I arrived home. As I walked into the house loneliness engulfed me. I double-locked the front door. Once I'd heard the sound of the key in the lock I felt my shoulders drop. I was so tense at work that I'd spent all day with my shoulders hunched around my ears. I dumped my bag in the hall and dragged myself up to the bathroom, where I splashed water over my face. Eye make-up ran down my cheeks. I was desperate to get rid of it, feeling it had become a mask I wore for work.

I walked past the living room into the kitchen. There was furniture in the house now, but the place was bland and unlived-in, a bit like a show house. I missed Ali's mess and the smell of his cooking. He made the best Irish stew and had often cooked it especially for me. But now the kitchen cupboards were empty. My stomach had shrunk and I hardly ever felt hungry these days.

I opened the fridge and took out a bottle of wine. I drank it fast and went to bed.

I found myself travelling almost every week to places like Manchester, Nottingham and London to follow up leads that never led anywhere. I was usually accompanied by another detective and had to stay in nondescript hotel rooms. Usually we grabbed a quick meal in the hotel restaurant then I retreated to my room. The quality of these hotels varied, and spending my evenings in strange bare rooms rubbed in my loneliness. The purpose of these trips was often to go to banks to look at financial transactions Blue might have been involved in and to get information from possible witnesses who might have dined in the same restaurant as him on the day he was murdered.

On one of my visits when I went to a bank in Nottingham to examine some of the transactions, one of the bank staff came into the office where I was waiting for information from her. She looked panicked and said, 'I'm sorry but I really need to tell you something. I won't be able to live with myself if I don't report this.'

'OK, go ahead,' I said. She explained that the man whose credit-card records we wanted to check, a GP, had been accessing thousands and thousands of paedophile websites.

'This has been going on for years, and I'm really concerned because he's a doctor,' she said. I took down some details and told her that although it wasn't part of our inquiry I would pass the information on to the relevant police force. The information was fed into a national police operation against paedophiles codenamed Ore.

As the months went by most of the officers who had initially been tasked with trying to solve Blue's murder were taken off the case and put onto other duties. In the end there was only DC Harvey and me left working on it; it was utterly soul-destroying, because every line of inquiry led nowhere.

Working on this snail's-pace investigation did nothing to alleviate my sense of dread that something terrible was going to happen to me in the police. The inquiry was like the state of my life, spiralling downwards towards nowhere. I struggled to get myself into work each day, and once I got there I didn't really have anything to do. All the inquiries we could possibly make had been made, but because it was such a high-profile murder the police didn't want to close the case completely. The family were still exerting pressure to find the killer.

There were many days when all I did was drink cup after cup of coffee, while doing absolutely nothing. I had to visit the family to tell them we were doing everything we could, but I found that harder and harder because there was nothing more to do and nothing new to tell them. But they continued to cling to hope, and kept coming up with their own theories to try to help us. Like our own inquiries, they led nowhere.

Because of this pressure from the family, the superintendent in charge of the inquiry asked us to recheck credit-card receipts that we'd already looked through twice. DC Harvey said, 'With all due respect, sir, we've already been through them twice. There's nothing there.'

He looked to me to back him up. Normally I would have been the first to speak out, but I felt too broken to challenge the superintendent. I sat quietly and said nothing, and we pointlessly rechecked the receipts.

During this time I became friendly with an undercover police officer called Ian who I'd known for a while. Our friendship developed into a relationship. He was a quiet guy, and didn't seem to mind that I was quiet too. He was the complete opposite of Ali who was loud and gregarious and full of fun.

Ian wasn't my normal type, but the fact that I began a relationship with him showed the changes in me. He was of average height and build with nice blue eyes.

I was finding it harder and harder to do anything. It was summer now and two years had passed since Alex Blue had been murdered. I was still working on the case although I was just going through the motions with my life at work and at home. I'd developed a rash and even though the weather was warm I was covering myself up. I felt itchy all the time. Red, scaly welts appeared on my skin that made me feel very self-conscious. I was now drinking two bottles of wine a night. Sometimes I'd drink with Ian – I was quite open with him about my alcohol intake – but more often I'd be alone. Both of us were working long hours and we didn't see that much of each other.

I'd cut myself off from most of my friends and didn't see my family as often as I used to. My clothes were hanging off me and I hardly ever washed them. The smallest thing I did took the utmost effort. No matter how much sleep I got I always felt it was never enough. I was exhausted the whole time. I had started to get flashbacks, often during the night. Sometimes I saw my mum lying in a hospital bed in intensive care. Sometimes DI Brady and DCI Harlow were knocking at my door, taking my fingerprints over and over again.

I was constantly weepy and I didn't know why. Anything at all could set me off. I was convinced there must be something seriously wrong with me but I tried to push it away. I was programmed to cope and just tried to carry on.

I was still waiting for some disaster to happen at work. Being stuck on the Alex Blue murder inquiry with no new leads was a form of torture. The inquiry was making no headway and I felt as if I was dying inside. I spent more time than ever looking over my shoulder at work because I had so little to do and so much time to think. The police's focus initially had been on the murder, but now that the inquiry had almost ground to a halt I felt more exposed. I was convinced that the lull would give them that much more time to focus on me, and that sooner or later the police would find a way to damage me.

As the months progressed my thoughts were becoming darker and darker. And then Ian was called in for a meeting with the Professional Standards Unit. He was an experienced undercover and drugs squad officer and was due for a promotion to the prestigious Scottish Crime Squad. He didn't think anything of being called into the PSU, as they sometimes asked him to do undercover work. But he was shocked when two senior officers began questioning him about me.

'What's her behaviour like? Is she erratic? Does she take drugs?'

When Ian looked taken aback one of the officers said, 'Don't worry, you'll only be confirming things we already know.'

'As far as Anne's behaviour goes, aren't all women erratic?' said Ian, thinking it was some kind of joke.

They kept repeating to him over and over again, like some sinister mantra, 'You're one of the good guys. You've been in the drugs squad, you would know.' Their parting shot was, 'Don't have any more to do with her for your own good. However, if you do carry on seeing her and you think there's anything we should know about, here's a direct number.'

It was scribbled down on a piece of paper.

Ian was horrified and immediately consulted a Police Federation representative. This officer contacted the PSU and was reassured that Ian was one of the good guys, that there were no disciplinary or misconduct charges against him and that this would be the end of the matter.

When he told me about the meeting I felt horror rising in my throat as if I was being strangled from the inside.

So this was it, the blow I had dreaded and anticipated for so long. It had come.

# Twenty-six

'I'd been dreading this for so long, that the police would get at me, and now it was actually happening,' I said to Dr Arbuthnot.

'So was that when you went off sick again?'

'Yes, a couple of days after Ian told me. By this point my whole body was covered in a rash from head to toe. That's when I finally went to the doctor. I burst into tears in her room. She said, "You've been trying to get by but your body's trying to tell you it's not coping. It's breaking down. You're suffering from a severe outbreak of hives and psoriasis." She referred me to a dermatologist at the hospital.'

'How did it make you feel when the GP said you weren't coping?' asked Dr Arbuthnot.

'I couldn't stop crying, and it was as if someone had at last given me permission to behave like that. I knew I couldn't cope. There was too much pressure. I was relieved that finally someone understood. I told her what had happened to me at work. She was sympathetic and said she'd seen this kind of thing before with police officers. She recognized that I was severely depressed. I was shocked, as I'd just thought I was tired. I understood stress in myself, but not depression, which seemed to be something far more serious.'

'Did she start you on antidepressants then?'

'Not right away. She was worried about me, and the first thing she did was to write me an eight-week sick note. She said I wouldn't be able to go back to work any time soon and that she wanted to see me regularly. I was also going for lots of appointments at the hospital for my skin problems. It wasn't long before I was started on antidepressants though.

'I resisted at first – I didn't want to take anything. I was worried about having the fact that I'd been prescribed antide-pressants entered on my medical records, because there was a stigma attached to things like that in the police. And I had my own prejudices against that kind of drug anyway.'

'Antidepressants are there as a crutch,' said Dr Arbuthnot. 'They can't solve all your problems but they can help you cope better with them. They work well with therapy and are there for just as long as you need them.'

'My own doctor made me realize that, and that people's attitudes towards them were down to their own ignorance. I tried lots of different antidepressants but many of them gave me bad side-effects like sickness and loss of appetite. I'm taking the antidepressant Effector at the moment and that seems to be helping.

'My doctor also recommended that I spoke to a psycholo-gist or a psychiatrist, because as a GP she didn't have the time to provide that kind of in-depth talking therapy for me. She was keen to refer me but said it could take up to six months to get an appointment. My family were worried about me and didn't want to wait that long, and that's why I ended up here.

They hadn't realized how serious things were until the signs were more visible with the skin thing. I'd covered everything up for so long.'

As I sat with Dr Arbuthnot I started thinking about my mum and dad. I had tried to shield them for so long from how I'd been feeling because I didn't want them to worry about me. They had always looked to me to look after them and I didn't want to let them down, especially after my mum had been so ill. But things had got to the stage where I couldn't hide them any longer. My illness was visible and I was off work. They'd suspected for a long time that something was wrong because I was getting more and more withdrawn. They'd assumed that it was caused by the stress of dealing with lots of difficult crimes rather than by what was going on inside the job.

As well as wanting to protect my parents I was too proud to open up to them about what was really going on. I avoided spending too much time with them, using my heavy workload as an excuse. When I was with them I was distant and tried to confine the conversation to small talk, the way I'd done with Ali. But I knew there was no way I could avoid telling them what the doctor had said. They could see how broken I was and it was a relief to unburden myself about how I'd really been feeling. Both of them hugged me and told me they loved me. They didn't really know what to do but seemed relieved that I'd finally opened up to them. They were used to seeing me as a tough, adult cop who didn't expose her emotions, and suddenly I was their vulnerable little girl again and they immediately swung into the role of my protectors. Although they were sad that I was so unwell they were relieved to get the real me back again.

I started to think about Ian too. Not long after I went off sick he was moved back to a uniformed job. Before he began a relationship with me he'd been promised he was going to the Scottish Crime Squad, but then things started going wrong in his career. He too found himself facing misconduct charges and is currently off sick with stress. He is unlikely to ever return to work as a police officer. This added to my stress because I felt I was responsible for messing up his career. If he hadn't been associated with me this would never have happened to him. I was very reluctant to take the relationship further with Ian. I felt as if I couldn't deal with his stress on top of my own.

'How did being diagnosed with a serious skin condition affect your self-esteem?' asked Dr Arbuthnot, breaking into my thoughts.

'I hated myself, I wanted to slide into a black hole. I felt that everything was against me. This was yet another thing that was going wrong. Around that time I got a call letting me know that my old friend Julie who I had joined the police with had been found dead. I knew she hadn't been coping a while back but I hadn't seen her for years. The news devastated me. At first I assumed it was suicide and I was very relieved when I found out it wasn't. She'd been drunk, had fallen asleep in the bath, and a stomach ulcer had burst.'

'Did you ever feel suicidal?'

'I never really contemplated killing myself. I don't think I could ever do something like that to my family.'

'You've been coming here for quite a while now, and I think that the cognitive behavioural therapy has really helped you. You've come along since you first came to see me but you've still got a long way to go.'

'One of the worst things for me is not understanding why this has happened to me,' I said.

'It's my opinion that you're suffering from Post-Traumatic Stress Syndrome brought on by a series of traumatic incidents. Sometimes this illness can happen if you've experienced one major trauma such as a plane crash. All the incidents you've been through over the years in the police have been traumatic in themselves, but all together they've culminated in this illness.'

I burst out crying, this time not with distress but with relief, because at last I knew what was wrong with me. Maybe this would be the first step towards getting some semblance of my old life back. I was overwhelmed, and struggled to take in what she was saying. I felt as if I'd been losing my mind for so long and that I would end up in a mental hospital. Just giving the illness a name made me feel normal again. The doctor explained that it happened to lots of people and had many different manifestations. But after the initial elation I'd felt from getting a diagnosis and finding out that I wasn't alone, I quickly sank back into gloom. I couldn't see how I was ever going to feel better and regain my old self. I felt as if someone had turned me upside down and emptied me out so that there was nothing left inside me. Fixing myself seemed impossible. I no longer knew who I was, and the carefree girl I used to be was just a distant memory.

'We're going to try and get you better, but you're going to have to think what you want to do about your job.'

'What do you mean?' I asked.

'I don't think it's a good environment for you to be in.'

I was shocked about what Dr Arbuthnot had just said about the police not being good for me. I'd never considered not being a police officer. Doing that job and the pressure that went with it had become a way of life that I hadn't linked with how I was feeling. My head was spinning. Now that I understood why I felt the way I did, I began to feel angry that this job had affected my health so severely.

'I don't think I can make a decision about leaving the police at the moment,' I said, my voice trembling. 'I don't know who I am any more.'

'There's no hurry,' she said. 'We need to build up your self-esteem first. Your identity's always been as a police officer, and that's what you're known as. You're probably feeling that if you lose that you'll have nothing. But that's not the case, it's just a state of mind. Your identity is Anne the person. It doesn't need to be Anne the police officer. I'm here to make sure you get yourself back.'

# Twenty-seven

Getting myself back wasn't as easy as it sounded. I couldn't afford to see Dr Arbuthnot any longer and so it was down to me to sort myself out.

I thought a lot about her suggestion that the police force wasn't a good environment for me to be in and gradually began to accept that she was right. I felt that I was good for the police but the police wasn't good for me. Then I began the long and painful process of disengaging myself from my employers. I was thirty-four years old and had given thirteen years of my life to the police. I'd been off sick for nine months and had been put on half-pay. During this time I had no contact with my immediate colleagues. Nobody called me or visited me. I was made to feel like a leper.

Since Ali had received that awful letter I had spent almost every moment waiting with dread for them to do something terrible to me, even though I was off sick. Physically I was several miles away from my old police office, but I still felt mentally controlled by them. Nothing sinister was done to me, but the conversation his superiors had had with Ian, their allegations against me, and what they might do next, kept preying on my mind.

My only dealings with the police during this period were with the occupational health section that I was duty-bound to visit in order to qualify for sick pay. It was very important to me that the doctor who was employed by the police could see that I was an honourable person and was telling the truth. These doctors have a reputation for being quite hard-nosed, but when I saw this man he waited until the nurse had left the room then said pointedly, 'I know what you're going through,' and smiled sympathetically.

He explained how I could retire from the police on ill-health grounds, and set the ball in motion, and now I was in limbo waiting for it happen. Severing my connections with the police was a lengthy process. There were four reports submitted to them in the end: one from Dr Arbuthnot, one from my GP, and two from doctors employed by the police. I was unhappy that I had to sign a form saying that I was unfit to be a police officer, because I felt that nothing could be further from the truth. That would stay with me, a stain on my character, until the day I died. But I had no choice, I had to sign the form.

Since going on half-pay, the social security had been paying me incapacity benefit because I was unfit to work, but in order to keep receiving incapacity benefit I also had to be interviewed regularly by a DSS doctor. It seemed that I had to constantly repeat my symptoms, something that just added to my stress.

About six months after going off sick I was sent some benefit forms to fill in, but my head felt so jumbled – as if it was clogged with cotton wool – that I couldn't make any sense of what they said. Even though I'd spent years filing complex police reports, now answering even the simplest of questions was beyond me, so my mum had made an appointment for someone at the DSS to fill the form in for me.

On the day of the appointment I walked up to the social security office in the rough part of Maryhill. My family were now the only people I saw. I could tell how worried Mum and Dad still were – they were constantly popping round to see me, or phoning me. 'I've made your dinner. Dad'll be up to collect you in half an hour,' Mum often called me to say.

I had no contact with anyone else at all. I bore no resemblance to the person I used to be. I'd been so strong, and now I felt too weak to do anything.

I reached the entrance to the DSS office and saw five or six drug addicts pushing through the doors and blocking my way. They were all men and they were shouting and swearing.

'Fucking move you prick, I was here first,' one of them snarled to another as he kicked at the glass door. I could see elderly security guards standing on the other side of the doors, obviously intimidated. When I'd worked for the police I'd often arrested drug addicts like them, but now I was in a different position, and like the security guards I felt scared. I suspected that like many of those I'd arrested they might be carrying weapons.

The guards pushed us all back outside and locked the doors. I felt panicked and clutched my handbag. The addicts looked strung out. I'd worked from the day I'd left school. How had I ended up here, waiting for handouts, money I couldn't even fill a form in to get?

A fight broke out between a few of the addicts.

'You owe me money, you cunt,' snarled a tattooed, greasy-haired guy to a skinny fellow addict. He stood back as if he was going to pull something from his waistband. The skinny guy, probably realizing he was about to be knifed, ran away. Tattooed Man turned to me. I had pinned myself against the glass door to try and put as much distance between them and me as possible. I felt helpless – I couldn't phone the police because I knew now that they were the last people I could trust to defend me, but I was terrified about what the guy with the knife was going to do. I had no protection, and as I pressed myself more firmly against the glass door I was sure something awful was about to happen to me, something I wouldn't be able to deal with.

'What are you looking at, you cow?' he growled.

I looked pleadingly through the glass at one of the guards as I stood numb with fear. Even though I was unable to do anything I could still read the situation. I banged on the door and begged the guards to let me in. One of them opened the doors a fraction to let me in, then shut them again quickly before any of the addicts could squeeze through. I had turned deathly pale and was shaking from head to foot. I asked if I could go to the toilet. I thought that if I could splash cold water on my face I might calm down.

'We got rid of the toilet because the junkies were using it to hit up,' said the guard.

I was obviously close to tears, and he must have felt sorry for me because he then said, 'I'll get someone to take you to the staff one.'

In the privacy of the toilet I had a good cry, then I splashed my face with cold water and looked at myself in the mirror. I didn't recognize the woman staring back at me. Who was I? I was no longer a police officer. I didn't have the comfort blanket of that job title behind me and I didn't have anyone I could talk to about what had just happened to me. I was nothing and I had no one. I was surrounded by darkness and the weakness was so acute it was like a physical pain. What had happened to me? I had built up so many skills over the years, yet felt I had nothing to offer. I couldn't imagine ever being able to do anything else and felt exiled in limbo. My body and mind were equally afflicted. I was in quicksand, and every time I tried to pull myself out I just sank deeper.

I dried my face and went back out to talk to the benefits officer, hoping he wouldn't notice my puffy eyes.

'So you're here for incapacity benefit. Have you left work?'

'I'm just waiting to be pensioned off from the police force.'

His face lit up. 'Why would you want to leave that? That's a great job.'

As so many others had done over the years, he was looking past me, Anne Ramsay, and could only see my job title. Now that there was some distance between me and the work I was able to see for the first time how much the job had defined me. Sometimes I'd told my sister Lynne off when she'd introduced me as 'my sister the police officer', as I felt it robbed me of my identity as Anne the woman. Even though I'd left the police I was still being defined by my former job title.

'It wasn't that great for me. I didn't get treated very well.'

'Oh, it must have been hard dealing with all those criminals.'

'It's not just the criminals. I loved many parts of the job

but I didn't love the institution and the people who controlled it. There was a lot of bullying that went on inside the job.'

'Right, OK,' he said, not wanting to get embroiled in a conversation about the shortcomings of the police. 'I'm going to fill these forms in for you. It won't take long.'

'I'm sorry, I'm just not capable of doing them. I've not been that well,' I said.

'Have you thought about getting a job as a security guard?' he asked. 'A lot of ex-police officers do that.'

I groaned inwardly. Nothing I'd said had reached him. Hadn't it occurred to him that I was too ill to work? I couldn't even fill a form in, and he was offering me a job. But what about when I got better? When I was with the police I'd done more than just stand by a door for hours on end. What on earth was I going to do now, if all that was on offer for me was being a security guard, a job that seemed to have all the worst elements of being a police officer without the interesting bits? Had things really come to this?

'I'm not ready to go back to work just now,' I said weakly.

I took the bus home, went straight out into the garden with my secateurs and began dead-heading the roses. Although there was hardly anything I was capable of doing these days, I'd become very fussy about trivial activities like making sure my house and garden looked immaculate. These things were petty, but they were the only tasks I seemed able to complete. My GP had referred me to a community wellbeing programme to try to motivate me to eat better and to take some exercise to make myself feel healthier. I went once but couldn't push myself to go back. Still, I did change my diet. I stopped drinking and started eating healthy foods in a bid to detox my body and my soul. I got myself a dog called Daisy, a cocker spaniel puppy who was an affectionate little bundle of energy. I adored her, and she made sure I got plenty of exercise.

For more than a year my half-life continued in this miserable way. Then one night my sister Lynne called me in a panic. She was writing a script for a film and was finding it hard to concentrate in her London flat. The pressure was on because her deadline was imminent.

'Why don't you come up here? It's nice and quiet. I'm not really doing anything and I could help you,' I suggested.

She jumped at the offer, and a couple of days later appeared on my doorstep carrying her suitcase and a bundle of papers.

My tidy, spotlessly clean house took on a lived-in look almost the second Lynne stepped over the threshold and flung her suitcase down in the middle of the hallway.

She looked around at my carefully polished worktops and plumped-up sofa cushions.

'God, you're anal!' she exclaimed.

I didn't stay that way for long. Lynne livened things up. She adored cooking, filled my kitchen with herbs I'd never heard of, and cooked me lovely meals like organic chicken curry. We fell into a companionable routine, strolling down to the village for a coffee every morning. Daisy would happily bound along with us while Lynne puffed on her cigarette and discussed her screenplay. We'd bounce ideas around and laugh.

I'd always been the practical daughter, while she was the creative one. Now I found myself looking after her, and that gave me a sense of purpose. I read the book she was adapting – it was the first one I'd read since I'd left the police. Until now I hadn't had the concentration to read anything. Normally I read books in just a few days, but this one took me a few months to get through. At least it was a start.

Gradually I got more involved in Lynne's work. I made suggestions about ways to make things sound more authentic. I'd stumbled into this work almost by accident, but found that I did have skills to offer. I had spent so much time with real people while I was in the police that I'd developed a good ear for how they spoke, and understood what sounded realistic. She trusted me because she knew I'd tell her the truth when I didn't like something and when I did. Lynne was impressed with the things I contributed. Feeling useful and doing some interesting work that was nothing to do with the police was healing me. I started to feel bits of my old self creeping back to the surface. The heavy black weight that had borne down so hard on my soul was beginning to shift.

By the time Lynne left to go back to London two months later I'd taken a huge step forward. My life had become meaningful again. It was going to take a while to get there but I was on my way to recovery.

# Epilogue

When a letter fell on the mat informing me that I was going to be discharged from the police on grounds of ill health I got a shock. I'd been in limbo for so long – I still felt part of the force even though I hadn't been to work for the last year and a half. Now suddenly it was all over. Fourteen years of my life had been spent as an employee of Strathclyde Police, and what did I have to show for it?

The letter explained that I was expected to hand back my appointments – my baton, handcuffs and warrant card. I'd left my baton and handcuffs in the police office because I'd fully expected to be going back to work. My warrant card had been my identity for the whole of my police career – it represented trust in me on the part of both the police and the public. Having to hand it back made me feel as if I was no longer trust-worthy and left me with an empty feeling inside. The next day I went to my local police station and handed the card in. As I walked out I felt bereft, as if I'd lost a part of myself.

Over the next few weeks I had a bitter-sweet feeling. One of the doctors chosen by the police to assess me recommended me for an injury award because he felt I'd been so damaged during my time in the force. I was awarded this on top of my police pension. It was important recognition from the police of how much I'd suffered while I'd worked for them. This too was a major factor in the healing process.

It was more usual for officers to get injury awards after losing a limb or being injured in a car crash whilst on duty. I'd never heard of anyone getting an award for PTSD. I received it for five years, although it's more common to receive an award of this kind for three.

There had been good times as well as bad, and I felt I'd given a lot to the police. One of the saddest things about the way things had turned out was that I had always received excellent appraisals saying that I had a lot of ability. Although I was relieved to be out, I didn't feel like celebrating. So much of my adult life had been in the organization and I couldn't imagine making a life away from it.

Slowly I began to understand that the police don't need to actually do anything physical to you to destroy you. The constant threat of what they might do is enough. There are no fingerprints left on the crime and you end up destroying yourself.

Ian, Ali, me – all of us good officers who if things had been handled differently would still be making our contribution to the police. Each of us gradually had the life crushed out of us until we had no choice but to leave the force. There are many good and well-intentioned people in the police and it's a really hard job to do. It's not surprising that some people deal with it by losing their ability to care.

I kept hoping, during my final nightmarish years in the job, that the chief constable or some other officer from the senior echelons of the force would step in, declare that things had gone too far, and put them right. But nothing like that happened. Things were left to escalate while the police machine ground mercilessly on.

As I reflected on my police career I began to think that there was not much difference between me and prostitutes like Margo Lafferty. Being dressed as her that night and being dressed in a police uniform, I sometimes felt I was being judged in the same way. Both of us had been filed in certain categories and were no longer judged as individuals.

By the time I left the job I felt that the criminals often have more integrity than the police. Whilst criminals are up to no good in a way that the police aren't, I felt that at least the criminals are honest about what they do. The police pretend to be whiter than white when in fact they're no different from everybody else. They hide behind their uniform, believing that no matter what they do it automatically makes them honest citizens and that they're above the law. The criminals I encountered had no truck with that sort of hypocrisy.

I believe that the police abuse the enormous powers they are given simply because they can. My journey through the police and my disentanglement from the job has been a painful one, but I have learnt a lot. I'm not sure that the force ever learns though, nor that anything will ever change. The institution that is the police is like a colossal steamroller, flattening any challenge or any voice of dissent that dares to cast a shadow over the way this monolithic structure operates. They recoil from transparency, determined to continue to do things the way they have always done them.

The police are skilled in manipulation. They drip-feed

information to a hungry press pack craving any nugget of information about gruesome killings and other major crimes. Even if the information turns out to be factually inaccurate or heavily spun, there is rarely any comeback, since the media is reluctant to bite the hand that feeds it.

I've come a long way since those days when I sat sobbing in Dr Arbuthnot's room. The panic attacks have stopped, I'm no longer on medication. All that seems to belong to another life. It's been a long hard road, but at last I've got myself back. I'm looking forward to the future. And I'm rejoicing because I no longer belong to the biggest gang in the world.